Real M. ~~~~ Arts for Real People

Choosing Self Defense that Works for You

Benchmark
Publishing Group, LLC

ISBN-13:978-1535188111
ISBN-10:1535188111

DEDICATION

This book is dedicated to all of the incredible professionals and companies who took the time to submit content to this book. It has been a pleasure working with each of you, in the production of this book. The time you have all taken and the high-quality content that you have all shared has truly gone above and beyond anything we could have ever expected when we first set out to publish this book. Thank you to everyone who made this possible.

Real Martial Arts for Real People

CONTENTS

Real Martial Arts for Real People

ACKNOWLEDGMENTS

Integrity Defense Academy

True Martial Arts

American Kenpo Karate

East Valley Martial Arts - Kenshin Kan

Marcos Duarte's Olympic Taekwondo

Aikido Eastside

Evergreen Kung Fu Club

Tiger Kim's Academy

Gotham Martial Arts

Pro Karate Center

Kumori Ryu Ninjutsu

High Speed Defense

Real Martial Arts for Real People

INTRODUCTION

If you've ever wanted to learn anything about self-defense, self-discipline, or self-control, studying Martial Arts is probably the first thing to come to mind. After you've thought about it for some time, you've all of a sudden come to the realization that there are many forms of Martial Arts, and you have absolutely no idea of which one to choose, or why.

The following information provided in "Real Martial Arts for Real People", has been compiled to give you a better understanding of a 'few' of the arts that are available, as well as specific interviews with instructors that teach these respective arts. The purpose of this publication is not to put one art over another, or to say one is better than the other.

The idea of this publication is to give you an overview of the arts available, and to provide you with detailed interviews with those that live and breathe these arts each and every day. After all, why would you want to make a decision about any type of physical training without hearing from the trainer beforehand?

Although there are many different forms of martial arts, they all have something very valuable in common, a genuine philosophy, and a primary goal that helps the participant to discover their inner self-control. Each style of martial arts has a unique discipline, that when studied over a long period of time, becomes a habit. True Martial Artists use this discipline in all areas of their lives.

Though this particular publication touches on all of these aspects, its primary focus is to help you make an educated decision on which art may be right for you. Some of the arts discussed in the publication may seem a bit time intensive and physical, while others may seem to promote thoughts, self-awareness, healing, and becoming in touch with an inner energy that is believed to be the driving force in all things.

With that being said, it's important to remember one thing, if you are specifically learning Martial Arts for self-defense, get ready to be surprised. We say this because regardless of which style you choose, if you make the conscious decision to commit yourself to the teachings, you will discover an inner strength in which you never knew existed.

As a beginner, there are certain items that will need to be considered and many of them will be covered in this publication. However, a primary focus should be placed upon why you are here, what you would like to learn, and how you will plan to commit once you've decided to become a student. As stated before, this publication is not about placing one art over the other; however, it is about providing information as to the differences among the arts discussed.

When we produced this book, we set out to find real world experts and that's exactly what we got. Our biggest challenge was getting these Martial Arts instructors to break away from their busy schedules of training their clients, so that they could actually share their advice in this book. The instructors who have contributed to this book "walk the walk", and the content they've provided, in the following chapters, will reflect their true knowledge and expertise. So, without further ado, we present to you, the real world expert interviews!

Krav Maga - Integrity Defense Academy

"Answers Provided by *Tonya Ben Mansour*"

*"I own and am the head instructor of the **Integrity Defense Academy**. We offer Krav Maga, Kick-Boxing, Wushu, Jujitsu, Karate. There are classes for kids, teens, and adults. I opened this school to create a place for everyone to have access to a broad spectrum of training. I personally prefer Krav Maga, but I feel there is something to gain from these other styles as well. I like Bruce Lee's attitude and Jeet Kune Do approach that there is something of value in all styles.*

I began training martial arts at the age of nine. Most little girls want to grow up to be princesses, but I saw my first Bruce Lee movie at the age of 5 and knew then the path of the warrior was for me. I wanted to grow up to be a master.

Training martial arts nearly my entire life, as well as teaching and helping others, is a great honor and a blessing."

Q.) Can you explain in your own words, what Krav Maga actually is?

A.) Krav Maga is the Israeli system of self-defense. It consists of hand to hand   Grappling Defense, handgun and Rifle defense/disarms, knife defense,   Stick, ax, machete, and other improvisational weapons defenses and disarms. When translated from Hebrew to English, it directly says contact combat. Krav Maga is a life-saving self-defense system rather than a sport martial art. Other styles of martial arts have sanctioned fights, but Krav Maga cannot be used in tournament fighting because the techniques target vulnerable areas such as the neck, throat, eyes, and other areas. It is not meant for games and sports.

Q.) How long have you trained this form of martial arts?

A.) I have trained in martial arts for 27 years. I have trained in Krav Maga for 3 years.

Katz presents me with Instructor certification.

Q.) How long have you taught this form of martial arts?

A.) I have been a Krav Maga instructor of IKI Krav Maga for one year.

Q.) Do you compete in Krav Maga competitions?

A.) There is not much out there in the way of a Krav Maga competition. I have recently seen, in the past months, a few self-defense competitions at karate tournaments. I am sure you could do a demonstration within that, but that would be the only way to "compete" using Krav Maga. The purpose behind it is not a competition. The purpose is to defend your life.

Letter of Appointment.

Q.) What is the relationship between Lmi Lichtenfeld and Krav Maga?

A.) Lichtenfeld Is the founder of a Krav Maga organization called KMW. Krav Maga Worldwide There are a few systems out there. Some good and some not.

I am trained and certified Under Moshe Katz, Founder of IKI, Israeli Krav International. I chose this system Over KMG not that KMG was all bad, I feel the weapons defense of my current system is most applicable to everyone and the knife defense of IKI are tighter and give the defender more control. Also, I feel our handgun techniques are safer than any I have researched.

My Wushu/Sanda teacher George Tsimpinoudakis and I, in Athens Greece.

Q.) What are the basic principles of Krav Maga?

A.) The basic principles of Krav Maga are simplicity and Fluidity. No movement should be wasted. The techniques are based on technique and should not rely on strength and muscle. In a moment of life or death, there is no 10,20, or 30 step Kata or Taulou. There is only simple reaction. When faced with a gun, you have a tenth of a second to react and you will not in the midst of flight or fight be able to think of some flamboyant 4 step move. It is one, maybe two actions. There is no more time.

Q.) What is the achievement, grading, or rank levels in Krav Maga?

A.) You start with nothing. And then yellow, orange, green, blue, brown, black and varying degrees of black.

Q.) Is this the only form of martial arts you teach?

A.) No. I am the head delegate over the United States for the Changchun Wushu/ Sanda federation Headed by George Tsimpinoudakis and Wenjun Wu. I am a Sanda coach, I teach Israeli freestyle kickboxing and in class, I blend elements of both as well as teach Krav Maga.

Q.) Is there a specific age group you are willing to teach with this form of martial arts?

A.) I believe self-defense is appropriate for almost any age. I see segregating classes between children and adults as necessary for training and general learning. Some of the topics we broach in Krav Maga such as rape, violent assault, and criminal profiling must be talked about differently to children and adults.

Some parents may not be comfortable with a very young child knowing about rape just yet. Mixing the training between adults is sometimes good and I feel necessary to show the child how to get away from an adult attacker. One of my students, a 12-year-old girl dropped a grown man 4 times her size escaping a Full Nelson in class just the other night. And it was beautiful. There is a benefit to mixing adults and children in training, but in general, there should be a segregated time in training between the two.

__Knife defense training in Israel.__

Q.) Can male and female participants become students of Krav Maga?

A.) Absolutely yes! I am a petite female myself and find Krav Maga to be the most effective way for a woman to defend herself, even against a man ridiculously larger than herself. For any man to defend himself for that matter. Anyone from a young child to the petite female, to the largest, most muscular seasoned warrior of men can learn and use Krav Maga. It is truly applicable to anyone, regardless of size, martial arts background, or lack thereof.

Gun Disarm training in Israel.

Q.) What should the prospective student prepare for before becoming a student of Krav Maga?

A.) The prospective student should prepare to let go, open the mind, relax, and expect to come WAY far from your comfort zone.   There is a risk of injury as there is in all martial arts. I would say less in Krav Maga. This is surprising based on the danger level of some techniques. Slips can happen anywhere. People get punched in all styles of martial arts. We train hard and smart to lesson slips and accidents.

In my class, we train as rough and real as possible without causing injury. Prepare to get some bruises. With repetitive bone on bone blocking and striking (especially in knife defense), there will be bruising. But it's nothing serious. I would rather hit and see some bruises in my Dojo than see my student dead in the street.

__Katz and I during training in Israel.__

Q.) Do you prefer Krav Maga over any other style of martial art you teach?

A.) Yes. Kickboxing is great fitness and a fun rough fighting sport, but Krav Maga is, "hands down", what has helped me in bad situations. Unfortunately, it happens. Kickboxing is nothing against a knife or a gun.

Q.) How often should a determined student show up for classes with Krav Maga?

A.) I teach Seven Krav Maga classes per week. Building muscle memory and split-second calm reaction are imperative in a study and proficiency of execution. I do not limit students on how often they may attend class. As a minimum, I like to see people on the mat 3 times a week.

Mat Training.

Q.) Is there anything you can add about Krav Maga that will help a student have a better understanding of this form of martial arts?

A.) Yes. In the IKI system, we teach the principle of A.P.C. - Ability, Purpose, Circumstance.

- Based on your ability, is it wise to continue engaging in combat or is it better to retreat and escape? It isn't wise to continue if you are a beginner or a seasoned fighter, but the latter stands a better chance prolonging the combat or fighting scenario.
- What is the purpose of the confrontation? If it is a common street fight, defend, diffuse and be gone. Is the assailant wanting your life? In this case, the purpose calls you to act and fight until the threat is subdued and down to the point of incapacitation.

- What is the circumstance? Are there other lives at stake? In this case, the circumstance calls to action the best of your ability because the purpose becomes that of saving the lives of others as well as your own.

To me, the fight you win the biggest trophy for is the one you don't fight, but we train hard so our fight will be easy.

If you would like to learn more about, Integrity Defense Academy, their information will follow.

Tonya Ben Mansour
Integrity Defense Academy
3990 Government Blvd.
Ste. E
Mobile, Al 36693
251-458-8884
http://www.integritykravmaga.com
kravdragon@icloud.com

Taekwondo & Arnis – True Martial Arts

"Answers Provided by *Skyler Zoppi*"

"True Martial Arts is family owned and operated in Sammamish, Washington by Laurel Zoppi and her son and daughter-in-law, Skyler and Angie Zoppi. We're a family-oriented martial arts school that was founded in 1982.

We combine a modern and progressive curriculum with traditional martial arts values. We teach two unique and complimentary martial arts, Taekwondo and Arnis. Taekwondo is a Korean martial art distinguished by its

long & low stances, high kicks, and jumping & flying kicks. The style is great for increased fitness, flexibility, balance, and coordination. Arnis is a Filipino weapons and close-quarters self-defense art. In addition, we teach practical, effective and usable self-defense techniques.

The scope of our program goes beyond teaching just kicks and punches. We teach our students to approach everything they do in the Black Belt Way, with 100% effort, a positive attitude, and indomitable spirit."

Q.) You may have been asked this a number of times, but where did Tae Kwon Do or Taekwondo originate?

A.) Taekwondo originated from Korea. During the mid-1940s and 1950s, Taekwondo was developed by incorporating elements of Japanese Karate along with ancient Korean martial arts mainly consisting of Taekkyeon, Gwonbeop, and Subak. The Karate influence came from Japanese colonial rule of Korea from 1910-1945.

Q.) What is the difference between traditional Taekwondo, Versus, Sports Taekwondo, or any of the other forms?

A.) Taekwondo in its original form is known as Traditional Taekwondo. Shortly after the end of the colonial occupation of Korea by Japan in 1945, new martial arts schools called "Kwans", were opened in the capital city of Seoul. There were nine schools in total. Traditional Taekwondo is an encompassing term that typically refers to the martial arts practiced by these nine Kwans during the 1940s and 1950s. It includes the powerful and elaborate kicks that most people are familiar with, but it also implements a wide array of hand technique, weapons and throws stripped from the modern sports version of Taekwondo.

Not long after the colonial rule of Japan ended, the Korean War (1950-1953) separated the country into two nations, the North and the South. The Kwans of Seoul were now a part of South Korea though some of the masters and ancient elements of Korean martial artists were rooted in the North. Being that the Kwans were established as separate entities teaching distinct styles, the South Korean government wished to merge them to form an institutionalized and unified style. After a decade of attempting to unify the Kwans, the International Taekwondo Federation (ITF) was formed in 1966.

The politics of the time and the bitter rivalry between North and South soured the relationship between the ITF and the South Korean government. Desiring to avoid North Korean influence, the Korean government abandoned the ITF and went a different direction in 1973 by forming the Kukkiwon as the official Taekwondo Headquarters of the world. The ITF relocated to Austria and still exists today, although fractured by political turmoil and in-fighting.

The Kukkiown established the World Taekwondo Federation (WTF) with the purpose of promoting Taekwondo as a widely practiced international sport. Kukkiwon-style Taekwondo is better known as sport-style Taekwondo, or Olympic-style Taekwondo. This version of Taekwondo took off and became an official medal event at the 2000 Olympic games in Australia. The Kukkiwon is also the home of the World Taekwondo Academy (WTA) which was founded in 1983 with the purpose of training masters to help spread the unified, Olympic-style Taekwondo around the world.

Since its founding, the WTA has produced over 5 million master instructors who have taken Taekwondo to dozens of countries, including all over America. That's why most Taekwondo schools in America are Olympic-style Taekwondo based. Still, Traditional Taekwondo and the arts of the original nine Kwans have also found their way to America and throughout the world via the ITF and the students and descendants of the original Kwans, who migrating elsewhere to teach their style.

Q.) Why did you make a decision to teach this form of martial arts?

A.) I didn't choose Taekwondo, Taekwondo chose me ☺. My Father, Thomas Zoppi, grew up in Reno, Nevada, where he developed an interest in Martial Arts and first started training in a local Taekwondo school under Grandmaster Lou Grasso. He then moved and eventually settled in Los Angeles, where he trained in Taekwondo under Sabumnim Dan DI Vito at the Choi Institute of Los Angeles in the 1970's.

Sabumnim Di Vito was a student of Grandmaster Chang Hae Choi at the Choi Institute in Chicago, Illinois. Grandmaster Choi is a master of the Traditional Taekwondo style of Chang Moo Kwon, who brought his style from Korea to Chicago.

In 1982, my Father along with my Mother, Laurel Zoppi, moved our family to Bellevue, Washington. He had to leave his training in Los Angeles with Sabumnim Di Vito behind, but never stopped talking about or practicing his martial arts. It wasn't long before I was begging to learn. As a 5th birthday gift, in October of 1982, we went out to the garage for my first martial arts lesson. The lessons continued and shortly after, a family friend showed interest and became Mr. Zoppi's first paying student. Word of mouth spread and other students joined including Laurel. In December of 1982, Thomas moved his lessons from the garage to his first rented location and True Martial Arts was off and running! Thomas Zoppi developed his own modernization of the techniques of the system. The new system was subsequently named American Chang Moo Kwan.

The school grew and thrived over the next 20 years. Although my Father passed away in 2001, True Martial Arts continued under the leadership of his students and his family. Graduating from college at that time and without a clear direction for what I wanted to do with my life, six months later I started working full-time at True Martial Arts. This was done out of a sense of duty to help my Mom. We had school managers, many loyal Instructors, and a Chief Instructor in place. My first role was just to learn about the schools from scratch and help out in any way I could. I worked at the front desk, became an Assistant Instructor, and tried to grasp the inner workings of the business.

As I became qualified and comfortable, eventually, I took on more roles and more responsibilities and became Chief Instructor in 2007. I feel so honored to carry on our school's traditions and continue my Dad's dream. But at some point, it became more than that to me. At some point, it became my dream, my life, and my purpose.

Q.) How strong does a person need to be, in terms of their leg strength, to perform Taekwondo?

A.) Taekwondo is a kicking art so leg strength is a big focus of our training. We also focus on increasing flexibility and building a strong foundation of balance in our legs. We primarily accomplish this by practicing everything we do in long, low stances (LLS). When we practice punches and blocks, we do these techniques in LLS. LLS isn't practical for a real self-defense situation. You don't commonly see people delivering real-life kicks and punches from a crouching, knee-bent, and feet wide apart stance.

But by practicing in LLS, we get the benefits of increased balance, flexibility and strength in our legs for higher and more powerful kicks. Being able to move easily from one LLS to the next shows our elevated levels of balance, flexibility, and strength in our legs when performing Taekwondo at a competition, test or demonstration. An advanced Taekwondo practitioner would make this look relatively easy and natural and it would be a way to set themselves apart from a beginning level practitioner.

Q.) How young or how old does a person need to be to practice this form of martial arts?

A.) A person could be as young as 2 years old when they begin and there is no age limit, as far as being too old.

When determining if a person is old enough to train, we look for two defining factors: 1) can the student stay on the floor and not wander off or lose interest 2) can the student obey the commands of the instructor and not be too much of a distraction to the other students in the class.

Admittedly, Taekwondo training is high-impact and can be difficult for older practitioners because of pain and soreness in the joints. This is especially so for your lower back, hips, knees and ankles. The jumping and spinning elements in the art can also take its toll or limit older practitioners. We don't expect a 60-year-old to be able to jump as high as the teenagers, we just expect that they train hard and progress to the best of their individual ability.

Q.) What are some of the key features of Taekwondo?

A.) Taekwondo is a Korean martial art, famous for its long, low stances and its high kicks, spinning kicks, jump kicks, and flying kicks. It is one of the most popular martial arts in the United States and the world, with an estimated 70 million practitioners. Physically, Taekwondo develops strength, quickness, balance, flexibility, and stamina. Mentally, Taekwondo develops courtesy, integrity, perseverance, self-control and indomitable spirit. Tae means "to strike or break with foot"; Kwon means "to strike or break with fist"; and Do means "way" or "art"; so Taekwondo is translated as "The way or art of the foot and fist".

In martial arts, the terms hard style and soft style represents how a defense counters the force of an attack. Taekwondo is a hard style. A hard technique meets force with force, either head-on, or by diagonally slicing through the strike with one's own force using parts of the body, such as the forearm, shoulders, thighs, knees and shins. Repeated repetition of receiving blows to these parts of the arms and legs hardens them and reduces the amount of pain felt upon impact. While hard techniques require greater strength for positive execution, it's the combination of power and the mechanics of the technique that accomplish the defense.

The training of Taekwondo typically includes:

Combat techniques emanating from the hands and the feet- Learning the fundamental techniques such as kicking, blocking and defending, punching and other striking and effective movements with your feet, to get you in and out of striking range. There are also more advanced lessons in technique such as adding stage motion to your movement, which is the ability to involve your hips and your legs to achieve the ultimate power. Another example is being able to relax while going hard. Between blocks, kicks, and hand strikes the practitioner should relax the body, then tense the muscles to make power only while performing the technique.

The techniques are often practiced in high repetition and then revisited frequently in future classes. Taekwondo training is not about learning a new technique each time and moving on to the next one. There is a basic foundation of movements that you practice so many times, that eventually they become natural and almost thoughtless to execute. This helps to make a practitioner more instinctive in a real life self-defense situation and less panicked or reactive.

Self-defense- Learning vital areas to target to defend yourself, ways of releasing and escaping from being grabbed or held against your will, foot sweeps and takedowns to get your attacker off balance or down to the ground, and step-spars, which is a prearranged defense done against an attack that is practiced over and over again.

Exercise- There are several different forms of exercise featured in Taekwondo training. Typically, they fall within this order in a class: **1)** Wake up the muscles, 2) Cardio training, 3) Strength training, 4) Interval training, and 5) Stretching.

Waking up the muscles is simply getting the body moving with motions such as arm circles, leg raises, hip rotations, neck rotations, etc. Cardio training is an aerobic exercise that builds stamina by performing your movement in a steady intensity over a long period of time. This could be drills, such as forms or kicks done in succession with high repetitions. Strength training and conditioning will be the building of muscle, typically done by holding low stances to build leg muscles, and push-ups and sit-ups to develop the upper body and core muscles. Many drills are Anaerobic, high-intensity exercises that build strength and speed by performing your movement in quick and all-out bursts of energy intervals. This could be like two-three minute sparring rounds, all-out kicking and punching on bags for a quantified period of time, or going all out when performing a form. Stretching is typically done after the muscles have been warm as part of a cooling down period to get your heart rate from elevated to regular and is also a great way to increase flexibility especially in your legs, hips and groin area.

Form- (called Poomsae or Hyung in Korean) - A prearranged sequence of techniques performed either with or without the use of a weapon. Most Forms resemble combat, but the emphasis is more on weaving different movements and techniques that flow together to be artistically pleasing. Form can be used as an effective conditioning tool and also as a way of demonstrating a martial artist's aptitude on many factors such as power, balance, precision, reality and correct technique.

Sparring- Free sparring is when two partners spar together for an extended period of time without interruption. Point sparring is interrupted and then resumed after each point is scored. Light contact with the body and little to no contact to the face is allowed in most Traditional Taekwondo sparring practice and competition. You are expected to be able to control your technique with precise accuracy and recoil the motion within an inch or barely penetrating into the person's targeted area. In most cases, you're safer to spar with an experienced and skilled Traditional Taekwondo practitioner than you are with a beginner or novice because of the superior level of control the more advanced fighter has. You should always have respect for your partner and look out for their well-being.

Board Breaking- A way to bring together the physical, technical, and mental aspects of your martial arts training. It can be used as either a demonstration of skill or a test of one's ability to deliver a powerful and technically correct strike (usually with a strike of the hand or foot). Mentally, intense focus and a clear and positive mindset is required.

Meditation- We learn to clear our mind. Don't let anything from the outside world bother you or affect your training. Push it to the side and be in the moment, so you can give 100% of your focus to your training. We learn to breathe properly through meditation so you can save energy and only exert yourself when it's efficient and effective.

Life skills- If you just teach someone how to kick and punch without the mental discipline to go with it, you could be creating a bully or a criminal. In addition to testing students on physical techniques for rank advancement, we also require them to memorize 4 phrases or key points that they must be able to recite and demonstrate in their behavior in class, which hopefully spills over into their everyday lives. Many Traditional Taekwondo schools will have something similar to this whether it be memorizing the tenets of Taekwondo or an oath said before the class.

For us, the most basic phrases are instructions on how to act in class, such as, "does not say negative things about the school or other students". It builds from there concepts that can be simple to understand, yet harder for some people to stick with, such as, "Self-motivated; works hard without being told to." More advanced concepts will be introduced at higher ranks, such as "Intention without reservation" and "Self-discipline, take action regardless of internal or external distractions."

Sport- The most common competitive aspects of Taekwondo are Form, Sparring and Board Breaking. In Traditional Taekwondo, the sports aspect comes secondary to the everyday training and lessons in philosophy. Because of Taekwondo's Eastern influence, the emphasis on winning takes a backseat to humility and being respectful to your opponent.

Q.) Is this a unique art to use for self-defense?

A.) Traditional Taekwondo is primarily a kicking art for self-defense when confronting an attacker. This is because:

1. You can counter-attack from a greater distance while staying out of harms way. The legs can reach longer than the arms.
2. The legs are the strongest muscles in the body. The world record for bench press was set in 2013. Paul Meeker lifted 1100 pounds one time in Bueno, Texas. By comparison, in 2015 a man named Jason Faulkner did a leg press of 1000 pounds sixty-eight times in one minute. If you've ever watched mixed martial arts or a Kickboxing match, often times you will see the competitors punch each other repeatedly with seemingly less effect, but when a solid kick to the headlands, more times than not, the match is usually over. We practice kicking high because of the numerous target areas located higher up on the body, including the nose, jaw, throat, temple, side of the neck, eyes, and ears.
3. Most people are caught off-guard when you defend yourself with kicks because they're not expecting to see them.

Some of the weaknesses that can be exposed in using Taekwondo for self-defense would be defending yourself from a close-quarters or clinching position, and also if the situation went down to the ground. For these reasons, I believe Taekwondo training should be supplemented by training that can address those weaknesses. Many modern schools, such as ours, bring in techniques from other styles such as Judo, Brazilian Jiu-Jitsu, Wrestling, Muay Thai, etc. to help their martial artists become better-rounded.

Q.) What are the differences between the World Taekwondo Federation (WTF), and the International Taekwondo Federation (ITF)?

A.) I'm not familiar with the specific differences other than what I previously mentioned.

Q.) What are some of the different promotions, belts, and ranks a person can achieve as a result of being a student of Taekwondo?

A.) A Black Belt represents achievement and excellence in martial arts. The way to accomplish this is through full commitment, being all in. It is not about doing things on occasion, when it is convenient, or when you feel good. It's about being consistent and doing what needs to be done to move forward towards your goal regardless of the obstacles you face. A Black Belt is nothing more than a White Belt that never gave up.

Logistically speaking, Taekwondo ranks are typically separated into two different groups. The lower-ranking group is the colored belts, also known as "junior ranks". The most common colored belt order you'd find would be a white belt followed by yellow, green, blue, brown and/or red belt. Each colored belt might have 2-3 stages before you advance to the next belt. This means a rank might be indicated by placing a stripe on the martial artist's current colored belt, not necessarily by earning a new colored belt each time they advance in rank. Each junior rank has a number assigned to it. The number depends on how many promotions it takes to achieve Black Belt. The number varies from school to school, but on average, it takes 9-12 rank promotions to achieve Black Belt. Junior ranks are also designated by the Korean word "Geup", which basically means "level". The number assigned begins at the highest number, depending on the number of promotions it takes to earn Black Belt. As you advance, the number progresses down towards the final rank before Black Belt, which is 1st Geup. So if it takes 12 promotions to achieve Black Belt, a White Belt might be referred to as 12th Geup.

The higher ranking group is the Black Belts, also known as "senior ranks". There are usually 8-10 levels of Black Belts. These ranks can be referred to in degrees, as in first-degree Black Belt. The senior ranks can also be denoted as Dan, a Korean word for steps. Under this usage, a first-degree Black Belt would be referred to as First Dan. So "first-degree Black Belt" and "first Dan" are interchangeable and both are correct usages when referring to a Black Belts rank. The degree or Dan is often indicated with stripes on the belt; one stripe for each advancement. But sometimes Black Belts are plain and unembellished, as many Black Belts consider it to be disrespectful to flaunt their ranking.

Rank advancement is typically decided by exams in which the students demonstrate their ability and recall of what they have learned before a panel of Black Belt judges or their Chief Instructor. Promotion exams contrast by the school, but may include such elements as the execution of form (Poomsae or Hyung), sparring and self-defense. Students will need to demonstrate the real application of the techniques they are taught in class while answering questions that show an understanding of the subject. A Black Belt test can be long and grueling, sometimes lasting several hours for more than one day. This can include a written test in addition to physically demonstrating their skills and abilities.

There are 3 main reasons why each rank may generally tend to take longer to obtain than the previous rank.

1) As you get higher in rank, Instructors have increased expectations of how well the moves need to be performed. To know what's expected of you, try to understand what the Instructors standards are for your rank.

2) The requirements and techniques become more complex as you get higher in rank. Beginning ranks provide a solid foundation by teaching basic movement. As you progress, you build on that foundation by learning techniques that are more difficult to comprehend and perform.

3) There is more to remember and improve upon. This is not only just the material for the current rank, but also from the previous ranks. Each new rank adds new techniques to learn. That means that with each new rank, that is one more set of requirements for you to practice and improve upon.

Be patient and consistent in your training and enjoy your journey. Earning new belts is great, but don't lose sight of what's really important in your martial arts training, which can be becoming proficient in self-defense or whatever goal you've set when you first started training.

Q.) Is there a genuine philosophy behind this form of martial arts?

A.) Do not strike others and do not allow others to strike you. The goal is peace without incident.

The techniques we learn as martial artists are to be used only as self-defense. The ultimate goal of self-defense is not defeating an opponent but rather it's staying safe. So the most likely way of achieving the ultimate goal of safety would be to not engage in the techniques we learn as martial artists at all.

A common question about this philosophy is "what if I have no the choice?" But you almost always have another choice because of several less-than-obvious layers to self-defense a would-be attacker would have to break through before you had no choice.

Having Respect is self-defense.

Respect yourself. When you show respect for yourself, it makes it easier for others to respect you because they see you as more worthy. If we are strong, healthy and take good care of ourselves, then we are less likely to be seen as an easy target.

Respect other people. Whether you are similar or different. Whether you get along or disagree. Whether they respect you or they don't. If we treat others with respect, chances are that we will attract some of the same respect back plus we will attract people and relationships that also place an emphasis on this type of positive behavior. You will be less likely to attract trouble or troubled people. This will help you to stay safer and put you in less dangerous situations.

Awareness is self-defense.

Attackers look for easy victims to surprise or take advantage of. To avoid this: Make eye contact. Be confident and walk tall. Don't look like an easy target. Greet strangers with a "hello" and give them a smile. Know what is going on around you, not just in front of you. Be aware of your surroundings.

Knowledge is self-defense.

Know who the people are that are potential threats. This includes:
- Someone making you uncomfortable, whether you know that person or not.
- Someone asking for help or offering some kind of favor out of the blue.
- Someone that tries to get you away from your family or friends, whether you know that person or not.

Distance is self-defense.

Don't let people into your personal space if it makes you uncomfortable. Personal space is within an extended arm's length. Keep your distance from people that give you an uneasy feeling.

Your Voice is self-defense.

Use energy in your voice. Speak loud and clear so you can be understood. Speaking loud and clear makes a would-be-attacker understands that what they're doing makes you uncomfortable. Being loud and clear gets the attention of people around you and alerts them of a potential threat.

De-escalation is self-defense.

De-escalation is the use of tone, voice, and the language of the body to set at ease a potentially violent situation before it takes place. If your goal is to de-escalate then do not: threaten, argue with, challenge, make demands or disrespect the aggressor.

Avoidance is self-defense.

Being aware of and avoid potentially dangerous situations. Keep your distance from potentially dangerous people, places, and situations. If something doesn't seem right, it might not be. If you're uncomfortable, that's your body's way of telling you something isn't right.

Q.) Are there competitions for Taekwondo a person can train for?

A.) Traditional Taekwondo Schools will typically hold in-house tournaments, tournaments with affiliated schools or participate in open-style tournaments. That's because most of these schools are independent and aren't affiliated with any large organization such as the World Taekwondo Federation or a common style such as Shotokan Karate.

Traditional Taekwondo sparring competitions are usually done with padding for the hands, feet, and head, but without chest protectors because only light contact is allowed. A point is awarded for any proper hand or foot technique that comes within approximately three inches of the target area. Physical contact is not required to score. Attacking techniques must be delivered with good focus, power, and balance, and must not be fully extended. Fully extended means that the attacker could not have reached any farther. Target areas include the front and sides of the head and neck, the chest, stomach, and the rib cage. A winner is determined by reaching a pre-determined amount of points first (usually 3-5) or being ahead on points when the time duration of the match has expired (usually one round lasting 3-5 minutes).

Forms competitions are judged by a panel of Black Belts. Contestants receive a score between zero and ten, using tenth points. Judges base their score on the following important criteria: Correct technique, Speed & power, and Reality. Correct Technique is defined as correct motion, balance, and posture. Speed and Power should show that the techniques flow together as appropriate. Reality means that the contestant's form looks real and that the contestant has a good presence in the ring.

Q.) What are the five tenets of Taekwondo?

A.) The five tenets of Taekwondo are:

- Courtesy (Ye Ui) – Be thoughtful, polite and considerate of others.
- Integrity (Yom Chi) – Integrity describes how you should interact with others. To be honest and good, earn respect and trust.
- Perseverance (In Nae) – Internal drive. Challenges allow us to improve ourselves and, therefore, should not be avoided.
- Self-Control (Kuk Gi) – To have control of your body and mind in your actions and reactions.
- Indomitable Spirit (Baekjool) – To have courage in the face of adversity. Never be dominated by, or have your spirit broken by another person or anything.

Q.) Do you teach any other form of martial arts? If so, why?

In addition to Taekwondo, we teach Modern Arnis. Arnis is a lethal close-combat system of Filipino fighting arts in addition to being the Philippines' national martial art and sport. Arnis is commonly both practiced with weapons and the empty hand. The primary weapon of Arnis is the rattan stick, usually made of rattan and approximately 26-28 inches in length. There are single and double stick techniques and techniques to disarm a stick if you're empty-handed. Other features of Arnis include the use of the 5-foot long BO, sword and dagger, two-handed long sword, Sinawali (memorized stick patterns), and Taipei-Taipei (joint locks performed with the stick). The empty-hand training includes strikes, defenses, traps, joint locks, and throws.

True Martial Arts students train and obtain rank in Arnis as they progress and obtain rank in Taekwondo. As you advance higher in the Taekwondo ranks, it's a requirement to hold the same rank in Arnis. Holding ranks in both arts is a significant distinction for our school. Black Belts at True Martial Arts will be Black Belts in two different arts that complement each other very well; Taekwondo is a hard style and Arnis is a soft style. Hard and soft, in martial arts, refer to the way techniques deal with the force of an attack. In a soft technique, the receiver uses the aggressor's force and momentum against him by leading the attack in a direction where the receiver will be positioned in advantage. By contrast, a hard technique meets force with force, either by directly blocking the technique with a head-on force or by slicing through at an angle with one's own force.

Arnis is a progressive art, meaning that the techniques flow from one to the next, inflicting more damage and gaining greater control of the opponent with each sequence of movements. For example, an attack might be met with a block, countered with strikes, flowed into a joint lock which might become a throw to the ground, which could then become an attack to a pressure point while the opponent is trapped on the ground.

Arnis was originally a bladed fighting art brought to the Philippines by the Spaniards. The use of the rattan stick came about when the Spanish, the Japanese, and the Americans controlled the Philippine Islands and banned the Filipinos from possessing weapons. They used rattan sticks to simulate knives and swords, and they added a musical element to their practice to disguise its martial arts nature. Because the Philippines consists of seven major islands and over a thousand minor islands, no organized or streamlined Filipino martial art existed for many years. The names of the routines and even the name of the martial art itself varies from region to region. Arnis is also known as Kali, Escrima, and Silat.

Remy Presas founded his own system called Modern Arnis. His goal was to preserve the common techniques from all sources and organize them into one system. He was able to bring about renewed interest in an otherwise dying art. He toured the world as a Filipino diplomat and an expert in Arnis, promoting the countries sport and culture. Later, he moved to the USA. He continued to tour the country and the world, beloved for spreading his art to countless practitioners, including True Martial Arts founder Thomas Zoppi.

Remy Presas came to Los Angeles in 1981 to write a book about Arnis. During that time, he took a liking to Dan Di Vito's Choi Institute studio in Hollywood, California and decided to stay a while. This, of course, is where my Father, Thomas Zoppi, taught and trained at the time. Dan Di Vito (my Father's Instructor), Thomas Zoppi, and another man named Pem Wall became his first West Coast Black Belts. The three of them, along with one of his Black Belts from a previous stop in Michigan, helped to put together the materials for his first book, entitled Modern Arnis. The pictures for the book were shot at the Los Angeles studios of Black Belt magazine.

Thomas Zoppi integrated Modern Arnis into the curriculum of True Martial Arts when he founded his own school in 1982 after moving to Bellevue, Washington. Remy Presas came to Washington to stay with us and teach seminars at our school many times between 1982 and 2001, the year these two friends both passed away. My Father wasn't the type to seek attention or fame in the martial arts, but I know the honors of being one of the first West Coast Black Belts of Remy Presas, appearing in his book "Modern Arnis" and to later be presented the titles of Guro and Chief Instructor for the State of Washington were some of his proudest moments as a martial artist.

Q.) Is there anything you can add that would help a person make a decision about studying this form of martial arts?

A.) While I have a great love for Chang Moo Kwon, Traditional Taekwondo and Taekwondo in general, I highly recommend placing an emphasis on finding a great school with an Instructor that conducts his or herself with integrity. The school should place an emphasis on being community-oriented and should feel like a second home.

What are the Black Belts at the prospective school like... are they someone you'd like to emulate one day? Belts and awards should only come as a result of hard work. Ask the instructor how long it takes to typically get to Black Belt. Whatever you are hoping to get out of the training, look at that particular schools, higher ranks, those that have blazed the trail before you, to see if they have what it is you're looking for or wanting to become.

It is my opinion that the school should not be over-commercialized by getting away from the core teachings of martial arts or by providing services that have nothing to do with Martial Arts. Is there a master instructor owning and operating the school or is it a hired-hand running a satellite school just to earn money for someone else? Also, is the school looking for a big financial commitment up-front? Look for references on-line about that particular school or Instructor. I've heard so many times about people signing these big contracts and putting money up-front, only to show up and find the school locked up and deserted one day. It is fair to ask if the school plans to stay in business well into the future.

Best of luck in your Martial Arts journey!

If you would like to learn more about, True Martial Arts, their information will follow.

True Martial Arts
2912 228th Ave SE
Sammamish, WA 98075
Phone: 425-313-9680
Website: www.truemartialarts.com
Email: info@truemartialarts.com
Social Media: Facebook.com/truemartialarts
Blog: https://gjnskylerzoppi.wordpress.com

American Kenpo Karate - MG Kenpo Academy

"Answers Provided by *Maurice Anthony Gomez Sr.*"

"Established in 2007, we started out as a private club in the garage of my personal home. Since then we have grown much larger, and we are now operating at a commercial school in the City of Duarte. We primarily teach American Kenpo Karate which includes Jeff Speakman's Kenpo 5.0, Ed Parkers American Kenpo Karate. Aside from Kenpo Karate, our school offers courses in tactical self-defense for law enforcement, Brazilian Jiu-Jitsu, and Filipino Martial Arts."

Q.) What does the word Kenpo mean?

A.) About 700 years ago, a fighting art was brought from the country of China by the Yoshida Clan, to the country of Japan, and quickly adopted by a clan called Komatsu. It was an unarmed fighting art called Kenpo. The word Kenpo literally means "Fist Law/Law of the Fist" and also refers to its Chinese origin. In Chinese, it is known as "Chuan Fa/Quan Fa."

Q.) Is there a difference between Kempo and Kenpo?

A.) In actual practice, if you were to watch a KEMPO stylist perform his/her art, you would probably see larger circles, lower stances, and traditional (and sometimes, impractical) movement. A KENPO stylist (especially an American Kenpo practitioner) would, in contrast, display smaller circles, a higher, but still very stable, stance, and very direct, powerful movement.

Q.) Why did you decide to teach Kenpo?

A.) I was always intrigued by the martial arts since I was a child. I have an older brother who took up martial arts as well and I used to go and watch his classes as well as go to different martial art events and see different people doing different things. It was fascinating to me. Growing up I tried all sorts of different martial arts styles including Kenpo. It was Kenpo that kept me motivated and made sense for me. I was drawn by the explosiveness, speed, and power that Kenpo possesses. I was looking for something that I know would keep me safe in the event that I ever had to defend myself on the streets or if I had to protect a loved one from a potential attacker. Kenpo gave me that in a realistic fashion.

Q.) Are there different forms of Kenpo?

A.) Yes. Among them are American Kenpo, Jeff Speakman's Kenpo 5.0 (a modern evolution of Grandmaster Ed Parker's American Kenpo), Tracy Kenpo, Ralph Castro's Shaolin Kenpo, Nick Cerio Kenpo, Chinese Kenpo (many varieties), Hawaiian Kenpo, Okinawan Kenpo, Kara-ho Kempo, Kosho Ryu Kempo, Kosho Shorei Ryu Kempo, Villari Kempo, and Shaolin Kempo to name some of the more commonly known ones. Then there are also related, Kenpo-based systems that exist, such as Kajukenbo and Karazenpo Goshinjitsu.

Q.) Is it true that Kenpo incorporates a number of different Japanese martial arts?

A.) Originally, Kenpo was known as Kenpo Jujitsu, and incorporated aspects of Okinawan Karate, and Traditional

Japanese Jujitsu. Much of the grappling aspect was removed from the system as it evolved, and eventually, the Kenpo we know and practice today is primarily a striking art. However, you are still able to see, within the system, that there are influences from traditional jujitsu (such as leverages, takedowns, and defenses to those attacks) that still remain.

Q.) Is American Kenpo and Okinawan Kenpo that much different?

A.) Yes. From my experience, Okinawan Kenpo embraces the hard, rigid movement common in Okinawan Karate. The movements are very linear and do not have a flowing aesthetic. It is very traditional. American Kenpo, on the other hand, is very practical. It is an evolved system of Karate that was designed for a modern type of attack. The movements stress proper body mechanics, body positions, the economy of motion, proper angles of entry and execution, and incorporate flowing, combination defenses, and attacks.

Q.) Why is Kenpo also referred to as Karate in the United States?

A.) Karate, literally translated, is Japanese for "empty hand." Kenpo, being the fact that it is a methodology of empty hand self-defense/combat is recognized as a system of Karate. Hence the categorization would be the ART of Karate, the SYSTEM of Kenpo, and the STYLE is American. So, you have American Kenpo Karate.

Q.) What is the minimum age a person has to be in order to study this form of martial arts?

A.) Every school has different age requirements for entry. Typically you'll see students as young as 3 ½ to 4 years of age starting to take Kenpo. These classes typically are called a Little Tiger or Little Dragon program. I personally do not teach anyone under the age of 10 any longer.

Q.) What are the basic physical and mental requirements to begin practicing?

A.) To begin practicing, for optimum results, the basic physical requirement is that you have 2 hands and 2 feet, and can move them naturally. Anything above and beyond that, a student must work to develop and/or maintain... such as their overall fitness level, their body weight, their coordination, dexterity, and balance. Mentally, a student must have an open mind, self-motivation, and an ability to focus. These characteristics will continue to develop, as will others, through the course of training.

Q.) How much time is required each week for studies?

A.) Time is always measured by value. If you find value in the martial arts, then you'll devote more time to coming to class. Some students come once a week to the class, some twice, some every day. It varies by the commitment level and dedication that student wants to put in. On average, you'll find a student comes in at least 2 times a week. This is usually recommended so that you can get a proper balance of curriculum that we have to offer.

Q.) What is the average time frame for a person to move up in the different levels of Kenpo?

A.) The answer relates to the question above about requirements of time each week. If a person devotes more time to come to class, they'll excel faster than those that don't come to class as much. This may not always be the case. Some are slower learners than others so the extra time they come to class may not be as beneficial than the person who's a fast learner, has natural talents and only comes in once or twice a week. We treat every person differently and don't force people to move up in rank if they're not ready. We like to motivate and instill the goal to get them to move up in rank, but only when we know that they're ready for it. Moving up in the ranks can vary in time. The beginner levels can expect advancement every 2-3 months. An intermediate student can expect advancement every 3-6 months. Brown belt levels typically are 6-12 months apart for advancements. Black Belt levels vary depending on the degree. On average, it takes an average student anywhere from 5-6 years to go from white to Black Belt in our system.

Q.) Why is Kenpo considered to be a unique form of martial arts?

A.) Keno is considered unique, because, although it was born from traditional roots, it has constantly evolved, over the years, to meet the needs and demands of a changing society of violence, and a changing world. For instance, 50 years ago, if two individuals were to get into a fist fight in the street, it would NOT be out of the ordinary for one participant to allow his opponent to get up off the ground if the opponent had tripped or fallen. That was just the mindset of the time. Nowadays, however, ground fighting is not only expected but the PREFERRED method by many trained individuals, as well as the untrained "wannabe" MMA spectators-turned-street fighters. American Kenpo has been often termed as the "Science of Street Fighting." This, as a description in, and of itself, is unique. It denotes that FIGHTING is part of the "self-defense paradigm." American Kenpo addresses this in a logical, scientific manner, using angles, lines, body position and body structure, and is taught in a manner unlike any other system of Karate. The late Sr. Grandmaster Ed Parker has been quoted as saying, "Traditionalists often study what is taught, not what there is to create."

Q.) Why are there so many different influences in the art of Kenpo?

A.) Because Kenpo borrows the BEST aspects of different martial arts to create a seamless flow of motion. Starting with its roots in Kung Fu, its migration to Okinawa, then being transplanted into Hawaii, and finally the U.S. mainland, Kenpo picked up countless attributes. The circular and linear movement, the targeting of the strikes and kicks, the continuity of motion, the devastating power, the scientific principles, among many others are all ingredients added to the mix as Kenpo passed from generation to generation, culture to culture, practitioner to practitioner.

Q.) Is there anything you can add about Kenpo that would help a person make a decision about studying this form of martial arts for self-defense?

A.) My advice is that you have to know what you're getting into. This is a martial art that can save your behind in the street. If you don't train hard and keep it real, it won't be there to save you. It's a lot of hard work, it's not magic. If you put in the time, commit and dedicate your life to it, you will reap all the rewards that Kenpo has to offer. In my opinion, Kenpo is considered a "University" of martial arts.

If you would like to learn more about, MG Kenpo Academy, their information will follow.

MG Kenpo Academy
Maurice Anthony Gomez Sr.
1740 E. Huntington Dr.
Duarte, CA 91010
626-831-6953
mgomez@mgkenpoacademy.com
http://www.mgkenpoacademy.com

Ryukyu Kempo – East Valley Martial Arts - Kenshin Kan

"Answers Provided by *Jenifer Tull-Gauger*"

"EVMA teaches traditional Okinawan karate to adults and kids in a family-owned, family-run, family-friendly atmosphere. Discipline, respect and character building are integral to the teachings of this effective life protection art. EVMA is a part of the United Ryukyu Kempo Alliance, and an alliance of traditional Okinawan karate Dojos, worldwide, founded by and under the leadership of Allan Amor Kaicho. The URKA website is www.ryubeikan.org."

Q.) Can you explain, in your own words, what Ryukyu Kempo actually is?

A.) Ryukyu Kempo is the "Fist Way" of the people of Okinawa. Ryukyu is what Okinawa was called before it was named Okinawa by the Japanese. *Kem* is *ken*, or "fist." *Po* is *do*: signifying an art or way of life. Ryukyu Kempo refers to the path of hand training used to preserve the way of life of the days of peacefulness. The *kanji* (writing) for "Ryukyu" refers to the Ryukyu kingdom and the *kanji* for "Kempo" refers to the way of life or the path that was followed by practitioners of the ancient life protection arts.

Q.) What is the association between Taika Seiyu Oyata and Ryukyu Kempo?

A.) When Oyata Sensei first came to the United States from Okinawa, he observed many styles of Ryukyu arts flying under several different banners. He tried to teach that all Ryukyu arts had the same base and background (same DNA) as they were all developed for the protection of family and country, and the preservation of the culture of the ancient Ryukyu people. Taika Oyata developed his own organization in the US and called his original group Zenkoku Ryukyu Kempo Karate Kobudo Rengo Kai (Rengo Kai signifying the headquarters or parent organization). In 1994 he started the Oyata Shin Shu Ho Ryu (an organization within the Rengo Kai) of practitioners who were graded and certified to teach Oyata Sensei's personal art and carry on his specific teachings, separated and personalized by his own life experiences. He later formed the organization he named Ryu-Te to define his personal teachings. Our instructor Allan Amor Sensei continues to teach Ryukyu Kempo and Ryukyu Kobudo because the focus of the United Ryukyu Kempo Alliance is on the root teachings of the life protection arts. This includes the physical techniques, the traditional values and the culture promoted by Oyata Sensei.

Q.) How long have you been a student of this form of martial arts?

A.) I became a student of Ryukyu Kempo right around the beginning of the century. At that point, I was a brown belt.

Q.) How long have you taught this form of martial arts?

A.) I have taught Ryukyu Kempo for as long as I have been a student of it. I was already an assistant instructor when our Dojo (school) started the transition to Ryukyu Kempo.

Q.) Why did you choose Ryukyu Kempo as a primary art of choice?

A.) The first reason we transitioned to Ryukyu Kempo was because of the people. It was apparent to me upon meeting them that the United Ryukyu Kempo Alliance was highly supportive of our Dojo and its people. They personally showed their support as friends and as brothers in the martial arts. The second reason was because we saw what highly skilled martial artists these people were and we sought to train for that level of skill. From the start, the Alliance leadership has demonstrated the ideal of a human being first and a martial artist second. This means that the practice of Ryukyu Kempo encourages and demands the practitioners' constant development of good character as defined by Sakagawa Tode's Dojo Kun. It teaches the need for one's heart to be pure: the idea that a good heart motivates a good hand. Students learn to focus on the exercise behaviors of good moral character, sincerity, perseverance, respect and physical restraint. Following those values of the Dojo Kun will result in a good representation of the tenets of a good human being. These teachings prove to be valuable to all students of all ages. They are not limited to the Dojo and can be used in all facets of life to improve one's life overall.

Q.) Is there a specific age group you prefer to teach with this form of martial arts?

A.) My only preference is to have a good mix of classes to teach in each age group in any given week. It's fun to teach younger students because as a teacher, I get to be creative with various activities that will help with their focusing and following directions, as well as basic technique. It takes a lot of energy, attention, and patience to teach these classes. However, with this age group, you see quicker progress. It is also satisfying to see older kids growing in the martial arts. They learn to apply the values in their everyday lives and are good at communicating how it is working for them. Kids want to have fun and to learn, and there is no reason these things cannot go hand-in-hand, as long as the expected level of discipline and respect are present. We treat our teen students as adults, knowing that they are adults-in-training. With adults, you can go into a more detailed explanation about exactly how to do a technique and why that works best, and they have the attention span to absorb it. Adults usually catch on quicker and the older students are more likely to really appreciate what we do and what they learn. So I like teaching students of any age who are willing to learn, especially those who do so with a positive attitude. I have had students of all ages with excellent positive attitudes.

Q.) Is Ryukyu Kempo an art for both men and women?

A.) Ryukyu Kempo does not discriminate between men and women. Both genders are treated the same in training and in the rank promotion. Since it is a life protection art, both men and women can become skilled in it. Ryukyu Kempo works with the body's natural motions. Stances and hand positions are based on where the body is strongest. It attacks an opponent where the body is weakest. Gender does not matter much when working from these areas.

Q.) What should a potential participant prepare for before studying this form of martial arts?

A.) Just know that it uses real techniques that do work and can be dangerous. Use the techniques responsibly, with the supervision of a competent instructor, until you yourself become a competent instructor, and then still use them--and teach them--responsibly.

Q.) Is there any physical requirement for this form of martial arts?

A.) There is no physical requirement. What we seek are students with an internal character or "good hearts." If that is in place, and the student has a desire to learn, we can work through the physical part. The techniques that are taught start out very basic for beginners and go up from there.

Q.) What is the ranking system for Ryukyu Kempo?

A.) After white belt and before Black Belt, there are nine kyu ranks which count down to the Black Belt (e.g. ninth kyu, eighth kyu, etc.). The first level of Black Belt is Shodan or first level, second is Nidan, and from there you continue counting up to 10. Traditionally, it would take a lifetime of training, studying and teaching to get to 10th Dan, which is rare and is usually awarded at the end of one's life. At age 16, if a person shows maturity and responsibility, they can qualify for an adult Shodan or Nidan and when accepting a promotion, they are accepting the responsibilities that come with that rank and with being a representative of their Dojo and their art.

Q.) Can a person compete in competitions with Ryukyu Kempo?

A.) Yes, there are competitions specifically for Ryukyu Kempo, and students can compete and do well in various tournaments. However, we do not require or push competitions. We and our students seek to hone our skills and learn this art in order to help others and improve lives. Unfortunately, competitions do not often set up this type of atmosphere. Instead, they can encourage students to get caught up in focusing only on winning points, beating the other competitor, and getting a trophy.

Q.) Do you, as an instructor, perform in competitions?

A.) I do not normally compete or perform in competitions. Instructors, like parents, have a responsibility to lead, teach, provide and protect those who follow their teachings and trust in their guidance. Ryukyu Kempo tournaments are usually held to promote the art, to fellowship and to share with other Dojos and styles. Tournaments are events which should provide a safe environment to teach and promote the etiquette and behaviors of a disciplined group of human beings. It can be an opportunity to teach the many lessons of patience, sportsmanship, respect, honor, pride, leadership, and contribution. It's not just an opportunity to win a trophy and attend to one's ego. Senior *yudansha's* (Black Belts') role in these types of events should be in contributing leadership, wisdom, and exemplary character. Instructors are usually asked to participate in the duties of assuring a safe and disciplined environment and showing an example of authority through experience.

Q.) Are there any age requirements for training?

A.) It depends on the Dojo or school. At our Dojo, we have a program for adults and teens, one for kids aged six through 12, and a separate one for ages three to five. The age requirements to get into the older programs depend somewhat on the individual. Our youngest students must be at least three years old, able to communicate with the instructors (as this shows a certain level of required maturity and participation), and potty trained (as this shows a certain level of self-control). We offer a lot of mixed classes where kids, teens, and adults train together. This encourages multiple family members to become students, which has the potential to create stronger practitioners as they have training partners at home and can reinforce the lessons in other areas of life.

Q.) Do you teach any other form of martial arts?

A.) Along with Ryukyu Kempo, there is Ryukyu Kobudo or the traditional weaponry of Okinawa. Our Dojo has roots in Kobayashi Shorin-Ryu which goes along with Matayoshi Kobudo, so we do teach some of those forms (*katas*) and drills.

Q.) Can you add any additional information that will be helpful to potential participants wanting to become students of Ryukyu Kempo?

A.) For years, before we started, my husband and I were just mildly interested in martial arts. When we finally gave it a try we absolutely loved it from our first lesson. Today we see how it has exponentially changed our lives for the better. So I always advise people who are even just mildly interested in trying it out. If Ryukyu Kempo is not available, I do recommend traditional Okinawan karate, and if that is not available in your area, go for another traditional style. A good traditional school will focus on and promote the most important values of the martial arts as found in the Dojo Kun. These things like moral character, honesty, perseverance, respect and self-discipline are the values that when focused on and used in everyday life will make it worth living.

Thank you...

If you would like to learn more about, East Valley Martial Arts - Kenshin Kan, their information will follow.

Jenifer Tull-Gauger
East Valley Martial Arts - Kenshin Kan
jenifer@evma.net
www.EVMA.net
480.892.4240

Olympic Taekwondo – Marcos Duarte's Olympic Taekwondo

"Answers Provided by *Marcos M. Duarte*"

"Marcos Duarte's Olympic Taekwondo is focused on promoting the sport of WTF Taekwondo, otherwise known as "Olympic Taekwondo", as well as self-defense techniques applicable to real life situations.

It's our belief that to be a champion, you have to train with champions, so while we cater to people of all ages, our specialty is finding the most athletically gifted youngsters, and grooming them into Nationally-ranked Taekwondo Black Belts."

Q.) Do you know where Taekwondo might have originated?

A.) Taekwondo originated in Korea; it's their national past-time, like our Baseball.

Q.) Is there a difference between traditional Taekwondo versus Sports Taekwondo, or any of the other systems?

A.) Sports Taekwondo, is simply that; it focuses primarily on the game, or the sport of Olympic Taekwondo only, which in Korean is called: "Kyorugi".

Traditional Taekwondo (or "Tae Kwon Do") focuses on the variety of elements which make-up the art as a whole, such as: Terminology, Tradition & Customs, Forms (or "Poomse"), Weapons, Self-Defense, as well as Sparring.

Q.) Is there a reason you made a decision to teach this form of martial arts?

A.) It's my passion; I'm a Taekwondo champion at both the collegiate and national levels; it's what I'm good at.

Q.) How strong does a person need to be, in terms of their leg strength, to perform Taekwondo?

A.) To begin, not so strong at all; anyone can learn and enjoy Taekwondo, so long as they have basic athletic abilities, like running, jumping, and lifting their leg into the air. However, it's my job as an instructor to effectively condition athletes, and help them improve things like flexibility, strength, and stamina, in order to perform at an acceptable level, which makes them happy.

Q.) Whether younger or older, what age does a person need to be to practice this form of martial arts?

A.) I started at age three. Therefore, my honest opinion is that there is no age requirement to begin martial arts training; it's a lifestyle more than anything else. As far as being older, well, exercise will never "not" be of benefit to anyone, so I encourage people of all ages to start. The misconception is that when you start, now you're suddenly on a journey to becoming a world champion, and it's going to be tough. Not true, it's not like you're joining the military; it's just a hobby. A normal rate of progression is to advance in rank (or "gup" which refers to color-belts) about once every three months. However, that changes when you become a Black Belt, to where it's annually, in correspondence with your grade or "Dan" (degree of Black Belt). E.g. If you're advancing from 1st Dan to 2nd Dan, then you must have had your first degree for a minimum of two years; if advancing to 3rd Dan, it would require that you've been a 2nd Dan for three years, and so on...

By the time you're a Master (4th Dan), you've been a Black Belt for at least 10-12 years.

So if you see anyone who claims they're a Grand-Master (7th Dan and above), they better have some gray hairs on their head, otherwise, they're pulling your leg. Grand Masters are generally older gentlemen, while the average Master is generally between their 20's and 40's. By that time, however, you stop caring about rank; a Black Belt is a Black Belt simply. I was crushing "Masters" in competition when I was a young Black Belt in my teens; so as far as "competition" is concerned, it's an ability that matters most; it's about talent, not rank.

Not to say that it shouldn't be respected; always respect Black Belts and those of higher rank than you; always. Yet, when you get to that point, and you're a veteran of the Black Belt level, then you really begin to realize this.

Q.) Are there any key features of Taekwondo?

A.) Taekwondo is famous for having the fastest, most explosive and dynamic variety of kicks, of all the martial arts. Our spectacular spin-kicks and jumping-maneuvers are the trademark of Olympic Taekwondo.

Also, Taekwondo is easily recognizable by the gear we wear, particularly the chest-protectors (known as the: "Hogu") which are either Red or Blue, the colors of the Yin & Yang within the Korean flag.

Believe it or not, the gear we wear isn't as much for protection as one would think. When you get kicked in the chest, stomach, ribs, or back, you really feel it. The purpose of the Hugo isn't really to soften the blow, but instead is to make a sound, a sort of "pop". This allows the judges to hear the strike and therefore confirm that a point was scored. One of the rules is that a kick must be "audible", as well as producing "body-displacement", meaning the strike has to jolt your opponent, in order for the kick to be considered valid.

Secondly, the head gear doesn't soften a kick to the face, not at all; its purpose is instead to prevent you from further injury after having been knocked out, as it provides a cushion between your face and the floor when you fall. It's common (especially as a result of a Spinning-Back Kick) that players are unconscious before they hit the ground, thus unable to break their own fall, which with that particular kick, athletes generally fall in the same fashion, forward & face-first, accidentally shattering their nose. Helmets prevent that by giving a half-inch of cushion at the forehead.

True Story!

Q.) What are some of the key benefits a person will receive as a result of practicing this form of martial arts?

A.) Flexibility and agility will both be greatly improved, as well as coordination, and strength.

For athletes already in the martial arts, "speed" is dramatically improved as well.

Q.) Do you consider this a unique art to use for self-defense?

A.) My honest opinion... If you want self-defense, go to an MMA School, or just study Jiu-Jitsu, or Muay Thai.

Taekwondo is a sport, it's not a "fight". While there are some tough opponents out there, and a fight may occur in the ring, it's really a fight within certain rules, and it's not like boxing where people are actually attacked that way on the street. I say, sure, if you're good at Taekwondo, then you can probably kick faster than the average-Joe can even throw a punch, therefore you may be able to handle yourself in the street. However, if you're an average-Joe trying to get a little tougher so you can hold your own; this is not the martial art for you.

Will you learn some self-defense? Sure, but very generally, and it's not the sort that's applicable as something like Jiu-Jitsu, against a bigger stronger person, who's attempting to either rape someone or hold you down and beat you in the face; it's just not. I wish people would get that...

Q.) Are there any differences between the World Taekwondo Federation (WTF), and the International Taekwondo Federation (ITF)?

A.) The World Taekwondo Federation is the governing body for all WTF, or "Olympic Style" Taekwondo in the world. It's commonly confused with the Kukkiwon, which is the World Taekwondo Headquarters located in Seoul, Korea. It actually looks like a stereotypical "ancient temple" of sorts. The two are close but are separate entities entirely.

The ITF is the same, in that it's the governing body for the traditional style of Taekwondo, however, their competition style is much different, commonly known as "Point-Fighting". Athletes wear no chest protector, but have on soft boots & gloves, while at the same time punches are included and awarded points.

In the WTF style, punches are permitted, but only as a means of wearing down one's opponent; they aren't awarded any points.

Q.) Is Taekwondo the only form of martial arts you teach?

A.) Pretty much, I mean, I teach Tang Soo Do, which is Korean Karate much like the ITF style.

However, that's only to provide some diversity in training. Repetition is key to becoming a champion, and training is not always fun, yet sometimes repetition can get a little boring, or monotonous, so it's good to change things up once in a while. As an MMA Fighter, on occasion I'll teach my students a bit of grappling, or explain the differences in a variety of similar kicks, such as the Roundhouse of Taekwondo, and the Roundhouse of Muay Thai; where one is executed with the foot, from a further distance, while the other is with the shin, at a closer distance; either one can be devastating to an opponent; however, or as my coach so eloquently put it: "Roundhouse to the face hasn't changed".

Q.) Are there any different promotions, belts, and ranks a person can achieve as a result of being a student of Taekwondo?

A.) It depends on the school honestly; different instructors provide different awards to their students to keep them motivated. I like to stick to the traditional rank system personally, I think advancing should be rewarding enough, yet sometimes, I'll provide my students with a star on their collar for certain things like say, they had an excellent training day that day, or that week, and showed great effort, leadership skills, or just improvement in general. However, between belt ranks, students often have what they call "Tips", or a stripe that gets added onto their belt. This is a sort of checkpoint en route to their next belt, which indicates that they're making good progress, and are on track toward receiving their promotion.

Q.) What is the genuine philosophy behind this form of martial arts?

A.) We go by what we call the 7 Tenets of Taekwondo; basic principles we hold in order to guide us as individuals through our challenges in life. They are:

- Integrity

- Concentration

- Perseverance

- Respect & Obedience

- Humility

- Self Control

- Indomitable Spirit

Q.) What are some of the competitions, if any, a person can train for?

A.) There are Many.

There are Local Tournaments which are great for simply staying competitive, or preparing yourself for bigger events, as well as several State and Regional Tournaments held by the two major Taekwondo leagues, the Amateur Athletic Union (AAU), and USA Taekwondo (USAT); both of whom have a National Team, that travels to competitions all over the world. When you reach Black Belt level, there are also big events to train for, such as - USAT Nationals, AAU Nationals, The Germans Open, The Pan Am Games, The U.S. Open, The Olympic Games, and The World Championships.

(Believe it or not, winning the title of World Champion, means more than winning an Olympic Gold; the reason being, that more countries attend the World Championship than they do the Olympics; as such the divisions are much deeper. You may have to fight 7 to 10 matches in order to take gold at the World Championships, whereas you'll only have about 5 to take gold in the Olympics.)

Q.) Do you know what the five tenets of Taekwondo are?

A.) There are seven actually, as I mentioned above, however, we do have 5 Codes...

- Loyalty to Country

- Obedience to Parents

- Honor Friendships

- Achieve Your Goals

- In Battle, Choose with Sense & Wisdom.

Q.) Is there anything you can add that would help a person make a decision about studying this form of martial arts?

A.) If you like action, this sport has it.

If you like high flying, and lightning fast moves, this sport OWNS it!

Also, unlike many other sports, Taekwondo has a really good guy to girl ratio. It's very neutral, unlike things like Wrestling, or Football, which are primarily played by men. In Taekwondo, girls and guys train together at the same capacity and compete together at the same events (separated by Division only, Men's and Women's).

Taekwondo's fun once you understand how the game is played; I think it has something for everyone also.

If you're an athlete, able & agile, this is definitely the game for you; it also offers so much more to children in particular than things like Baseball, or Soccer, etc., The sense of community in Taekwondo is greater I think, and parents love to see their kids WIN. You don't bring home a 6ft Trophy or a Gold Medal in Baseball, or Soccer; there's one trophy only, and it goes to the team, usually placed somewhere that it's forgotten about as the years go by. You'll never want to stop bringing home 6ft Trophies, however, they're just too cool, it's too good a feeling, and sometimes, just sometimes, you can even win MONEY along with that trophy. You can't beat it.

Thank you...

If you would like to learn more about, Marcos Duarte's Olympic Taekwondo, their information will follow.

I can be contacted through email at, Blackmountainenterprise@gmail.com, or you can also find me on YouTube under the name: MartialDuartist.

If you'd like to watch my videos, simply type in, "Marcos Duarte Taekwondo" and I hope you enjoy!

Marcos M. Duarte
Marcos Duarte's Olympic Taekwondo
Blackmountainenterprise@gmail.com
YouTube: MartialDuartist
609.538.1700

Chapter 6

Aikido - Aikido Eastside

"Answers Provided by *George S Ledyard*"

Q.) How long have you taught Aikido?

A.) I started Aikido training in 1976 at the then newly opened Dojo In Washington, DC founded by Mitsugi Saotome Sensei; so that's 36 years.

Q.) What is the association with Aikido and Morihei Ueshiba?

A.) Morihei Ueshiba was my own teacher's teacher. He died in 1969 and is generally considered to be the Founder of Aikido. There are styles that use the name "Aikido" that are not in the Ueshiba lineage such as Nihon Goshin Aikido, but they are really not considered mainstream Aikido as their techniques are quite different.

Q.) Where did Aikido originate?

A.) Morihei Ueshiba created Aikido in Japan after training in a number of martial arts from the mid 1920's until WWII. The parent art is considered to be Daito Ryu Aikijujutsu and the Aikido Founder's teacher was a man named Takeda Sokaku. The Founder put the final touches on what would become modern Aikido while living in Iwama on his farm in the country during the late 1940's and early 1950's. In the post war period, teachers were sent out from the Headquarters Dojo in Tokyo around the world to spread the art. Koichi Tohei Sensei brought Aikido to the United States, first in Hawaii and then to the mainland in the late 1950's.

Q.) Why did you decide to teach Aikido?

A.) I loved the art of Aikido from the first time I saw it at a demonstration in Washington, DC put on by Saotome Sensei to promote his newly opened Dojo. I started training and there were 8 or so new beginners in my group and five Black Belts who had moved to DC to help Saotome Sensei open his school. Sensei flatly stated that he was training "professional teachers". It never occurred to me to question that. So, I always knew I would teach... right from the start.

Q.) Why does the art of Aikido require a uke and nage?

A.) Aikido is fundamentally the study of the connection. While there are certainly solo exercises that can be done, the basic practice is done paired. Rather than have a practice that degenerates into some sort of sparring, one person is designated to initiate an attack, the uke, and the partner, the nage, practices how to join with the attack and redirect it. The practice is designed to isolate and allow focus on the central principles of non-resistance and connection.

Q.) How old does a person have to be in order to begin studying Aikido?

A.) Any one person of any age can practice this art. Certainly a younger person trains more energetically or more physically than an older person. But very little in Aikido can't be done slower and softer and any person can find the practice fulfilling.

Q.) Does your school teach all ages? If not, why?

A.) We start children at the age of 7 currently. We have had classes for younger children, five and up, but we do not currently have an instructor for the youngest children. So we have classes for young people from age 7 to 14 or 15 when, as teens, the young people are ready to train with the adults.

Q.) What is the philosophy behind Aikido?

A.) There is a basic non-violent philosophy which is the underlying focus of Aikido. The techniques of the art are basically intended to control an attacker without unnecessary injury. The practice of the art is non-competitive and is really meant to be a practice of personal development rather than a fighting style. The Founder truly felt that the principles of Aikido could be transformative, both for the individual and for the society. The practice is about Peace rather than fighting. While it is an effective form of self defense, it is really meant to be a form of moving meditation.

Q.) Is this form of martial arts for self defense?

A.) Aikido is especially well suited for law enforcement and security personnel as it allows defense with minimum injury to the subject. For the average citizen, it is the long road to self defense capability. While it can be a very effective art, it is also one of the most complex and can take years of dedication to become very good. Most folks pursue the art because they love it and find the practice itself fulfilling rather than out of some need for street self defense.

Q.) What are some of the basic techniques of Aikido?

A.) The techniques of Aikido can be divided into basic categories. There are locking / controlling techniques for restraint. There are throwing techniques, some of which simply unbalance an opponent and allow them to take a front or back roll and others which involve actually "flipping" an opponent, which will require a better falling ability.

Q.) What are some of the initial attacks?

A.) The attacks of Aikido are quite stylized. There are three basic strikes: a vertical cut to the front of the head with the edge of the hand, an angle cut to the head with the edge of the hand, and a high or low punch. These attacks cover energy coming down on you vertically, energy coming at you from off the line of attack, and linear energy coming straight on the line of attack.

Q.) What are some of the weapons used in Aikido?

A.) While any weapon could be used utilizing Aikido principles, the traditional weapons are sword and staff. The practice weapons are usually wooden weapons making the practice safer. I was taught that there is no real distinction between weapons practice and empty hand practice. The principles should be the same. However, I think that weapons training is very important because weapons work can be done at a very high level of intensity even by older practitioners who are too old to train as physically as they had when young.

Q.) Why is mental training so important?

A.) The whole purpose of Aikido is mental training. The first movement in a martial interaction is that of the mind. So, the ability to join with an attack starts with proper perception of the intent of an attacker. Also, the techniques of Aikido are based on the ability to organize ones physical structure without using muscle tension. This depends on using the intent to activate the connective tissue of the body, the ligaments, tendons, and fascia and provide structure. This is why the art seems relaxed and soft while actually being quite powerful.

Q.) Can you explain about the uniforms required and the ranking?

A.) Most styles of Aikido wear practice uniforms called keiko gis. Additionally, what appears to be a skirt but is really a kind of baggy culottes, is worn. This is called a 'Hakama' and was the traditional dress of the samurai. The older traditional Japanese martial arts almost always wear these as do modern arts like Aikido, Kendo, Kyudo, Iaiado, etc.

Q.) Can you add any additional information about Aikido that would help a person understand more about this effective form of martial arts?

A.) Aikido practice is designed to develop a calm, centered, and relaxed attitude towards the various conflicts of daily life. While most people will probably never use a technique for actual self defense, everyone has to deal with conflict in every area of our lives. Aikido is a great practice for daily life.

Thank you...

If you would like to learn even more about, Aikido Eastside their information will follow.

George S Ledyard
Aikido Eastside
aikigeorge@aikieast.com
www.aikieast.com
www.aikidoforchildren.com
www.AikidoDvds.Com
425.802.3125

Kung Fu - Evergreen Kung Fu Club

"Answers Provided by *Keith Judelman*"

"The Evergreen Kung Fu Club provides private and group instruction to adults, children, and seniors in Kung fu, tai chi, Qigong (Chinese yoga), Shuai Chiao (kung fu grappling/ throwing), and self defense. We provide a supportive environment to help our students achieve physical fitness, internal strength, self discipline, focus, balance, coordination, self defense, and other skills to navigate life's challenges."

Q.) How long have you taught Kung Fu?

A.) I have taught Kung fu since 2008, though I only opened my first official school in 2010. I began studying in 1998.

Q.) What are the differences in Kung Fu, Gung Fu, and Wushu?

A.) Kung Fu and Gung Fu are different spellings for the same thing. Literally, kung/ gung means work, and fu means effort. To practice Kung fu is to put in a sustained effort over time honing a skill. We usually associate this idea with martial arts, but there is an aspect of Kung fu in the mastery of any skill, such as music, cooking, art or anything else. Wushu means martial arts, or more specifically it refers to Chinese martial arts.

In more pragmatic terms, Kung fu is a broad genre that includes martial arts of Chinese origins that can be differentiated into sport and martial (or self defense) categories. Competitions may include open hand or weapons forms, various forms of sparring such as Sanda (Chinese kickboxing), Sanshou, Shuai Chiao, continuous sparring etc.,.

Wushu in competition is more focused on forms as a performance art. Wushu forms are often quite elaborate, acrobatic, and flowery, sometimes set to music. Wushu would be closer to what we might find in the dramatic Kung fu movies coming out of China in the past several years.

If you are looking for sport or self defense, I would recommend Kung fu. If you are looking for beautiful performance art, acrobatics, and more of a gymnastic approach try Wushu. Both are difficult and will give you a fun, challenging workout.

Q.) Where did Kung Fu originate?

A.) Kung Fu originated in the geographical region today known as China, though one could also say that its influences stretch across east Asia. Originally different villages and regions had their own styles and over the years some styles grew and came to dominate and others remained small and others perished. During the cultural revolution a lot of traditional culture in China was destroyed and this includes a lot of martial arts heritage. A lot of people also fled during this period and spread Chinese martial traditions around the world.

Q.) Why did you decide to teach Kung Fu?

A.) I have found the practice of kung fu in my own life to be one of the best things I ever decided to do. It has helped me stay fit and healthy, it is a fun and interesting way of working out (you'll never find me in a gym or running, they don't work for me), and on top of self defense techniques it has taught me discipline, balance, focus, and how to cultivate my will (as in willpower). I am grateful to my teachers for all they have taught me, and I felt a responsibility to pass on what I have learned to others so that this special art can continue to survive and grow, and more people can benefit from its lessons.

Q.) Why is the art of Kung Fu considered a temple-based martial art?

A.) I personally don't consider kung fu to be a temple-based martial art, but to answer your question it is because the relationship between the Buddhist monks of the Shaolin temple and kung fu has become iconic in pop culture and movies. There is a long tradition of Kung fu being practiced in the Shaolin temples, but Kung fu is older than that and has roots in many places.

Q.) How old does a person have to be in order to begin studying Kung Fu?

A.) I don't think a person should be learning any martial arts under the age of 8, and this is in accord with my teachers and several other instructors I have spoken with. The reason is that we are talking about a martial art, which by definition is dealing with violence and there is a lot of potential trouble in teaching techniques to a child who doesn't understand the consequences of his actions. The next thing you know he is on the playground and does something serious to his friend and you've got a problem.

That being said, there are aspects of kung fu training methods that help develop balance, coordination, and focus which can be beneficial to younger kids (see next question for more on this).

Q.) Does your school teach all ages? If not, why?

A.) We have gone back and forth on this because there are a lot of young children in the neighborhood who are interested in kung fu even though they are only 4 or 5 years old. At the moment we have a class for 4-7 year olds that is about balance and coordination but doesn't really get into self defense; a class for kids 8-13 which focuses on developing good fitness habits, focus, discipline, coordination, and does get into self defense; an adult class which is focused on conditioning and self defense drawing on my lineage's military background; and a Tai Chi / Qigong class which is geared for seniors and people with limited mobility.

Q.) What is the philosophy behind Kung Fu?

A.) I don't know that there is one correct answer to this question and my guess is that every practitioner will give you their own answer. I would say that kung fu is about putting in a sustained effort in cultivating one's body and one's mind. It requires and builds focus and discipline, and mastery takes daily dedication. We need to talk about yin and yang if we want to talk about philosophy. Yin is the soft, receptive, accepting, the lower. Yang is the hard, active, engaging, the upper. We can analyze kung fu training and techniques using yin-yang theory and see the yang (strength training, strikes and kicks, attacks etc), the yin (suppleness, evasion, retreat, meditation etc), and the transformations between them (the dynamics of combat, a throw turning an opponent's yang into my own, using yin to redirect their yang, meeting yang with yang etc). I would also say that broadly speaking kung fu likes circles and spirals more than straight lines.

Q.) Is this form of martial arts for self defense?

A.) Yes, with the caveat that there are a lot of different schools of kung fu which may have their own goals or objectives. Some people use it for exercise, some for the performance art, some for sport, and some for military and police application (self defense). It is important to figure out what you want, and then find a good school or instructor who will provide that type of program.

Q.) What are some of the basics of Kung Fu?

A.) Kung fu techniques fall under the categories of *da* or upper body striking such as punching, *ti* or lower body striking such as kicks etc, *qin na* meaning joint locking/ submission/ seizing, *shuai* meaning throws. Training can include basic techniques, footwork, forms (sequences of techniques), Qigong (such as stances, isometrics, breathing exercises), calisthenics, weights, and the use of other tools such as bags, bars, belts, etc.,. My classes generally consist of some warm ups, stances and other conditioning, basic techniques, form practice, and partner drills that work on reflexes and practicing applications. Because of my Shuai Chiao background I also like to teach about how to land safely from a fall/ throw.

Q.) Why is meditation such an important aspect of this Chinese martial art?

A.) It is possible to practice Kung fu without meditation, but this becomes an external practice. By adding meditation, meaning a focused awareness and breathing coordination, one aligns the internal world (the mind or spirit or will) with the body's practice. This becomes what is called dual cultivation, simultaneous cultivation of the body and the mind.

Q.) How does a person train internal and external?

A.) A person trains internal by focusing on what one does, using mindfulness and breath work to engage the internal world. A person trains external by using and training the body. There is another way of using these terms. Internal combat is close combat, using throws and grappling (Shuai Chiao, Qin na). External combat happens from the outside, strikes and kicks. It is important to train both of these aspects (the yin and yang) because a live situation is dynamic and flows from one to the other.

Q.) Why will stance and posture be so important?

A.) Stances are a type of hard Qigong, which is one of the training methods that I believe are distinctive to Kung fu (though there may be aspects of this in other arts that I am unaware of). Stances done correctly are a form of dual cultivation. They simultaneously condition the body and build will power in a safe, effective manner. They build particular muscle groups that are important in the practice and application of Kung fu. They help detoxify the body through sweat and improve circulation.

Posture is important because if we have incorrect posture our body is not able to express its full potential. If I do a throw with correct posture, I can use all of my body's power. If my posture is incorrect, there will be a break in the chain and I will not be able to harness all of my power into my technique. Depending on what the problem is, I might be accessing 75% or even only 40% of my potential. There are also other long term problems that can arise from bad posture that we all know about (arthritis, degenerative joints, pain, tense shoulders/ neck etc.).

Q.) Can you explain the inner energy or Qi?

A.) Qi, or vital energy, is not as mysterious as we sometimes think. It is just the energy our body uses to move and function. Our blood circulates around our body, but Qi is what we call the energy that moves the blood, what makes our heart pump. Our organs function, and Qi is the energy that makes the functions happen. We are like a computer, and Qi is like the electricity that allows our body to turn on and operate.

Q.) Do you teach any other forms of martial arts? Please explain what they are and why?

A.) I teach a family of Chinese martial arts: traditional Kung fu (with some northern Shaolin roots) which we have been talking about; hard and soft Qigong which means stances, postures, meditations, breath work, isometrics, and simple movements. Hard Qigong to cultivate yang Qi such as power and will, and soft Qigong to cultivate yin aspects such as relaxation, suppleness, and health. Tai chi, which is a martial art practiced at a slow tempo combining martial techniques and soft Qigong which is great for reducing stress and as exercise for seniors and other people with limited mobility (obese, injured etc.). And Shuai Chiao which is the throwing/grappling part of kung fu. Together, these arts complement each other and provide cross-training of yin and yang cultivation. They build strength and train a range of martial techniques, develop coordination, focus, and will, and teach one to be supple and relaxed. It is easy to just train one aspect, but we need balance in our life to thrive. These arts also give people tools to train through every stage of life.

Q.) Can you add any additional information about Kung Fu that would help a person understand more about this ancient but extremely effective martial art?

A.) The most important thing is to find an activity that we like which is challenging and engaging, and to find a good school with a good instructor. We also need to figure out what it is we are looking for (fitness, sport, self defense etc.). This way we will be able to stick with it and develop and cultivate our art and skills and our self. Kung fu takes dedication. The saying "10,000 times makes a master" comes from Kung fu. Otherwise we may end up wasting our time or develop bad habits or a bad relationship to our exercise (I don't like the teacher so I don't like to go, it's not fun so I don't like to practice, the students aren't sensitive to each other so I get hurt when I practice so I don't go often, I'm not getting what I want out of this school so I'm going to give up altogether). Take some time to find a good instructor because it makes a huge difference. For years I had to drive 85 miles to go to class, but I did it because I had a great instructor. I'll leave you with one detail to look for in visiting prospective schools: watch the feet of the students who have been there a while when they do their horse stance. The toes should be straight ahead or slightly inward, not pointing outward.

Thank you...

If you would like to learn even more about, Evergreen Kung Fu Club, their information will follow.

Keith Judelman
Evergreen Kung Fu Club
info@EvergreenKungfu.com
www.EvergreenKungfu.com
206.419.3868

Tang Soo Do - Tiger Kim's Academy

"Answers Provided By *Grandmaster Tiger Kim*"

"Tiger Kim's Academy since 1976, has incorporated the three major Korean martial arts of Taekwondo, Tang Soo Do and Hapkido. Founded by Grandmaster Tiger Kim, the school reflects his many years of diverse martial arts training.

Taekwondo and Tang Soo Do are the main components and the primary focus at Tiger Kim's which certifies Black Belts throughout the world from its headquarters in Seoul, Korea (The Kukkiwon). Literally, Taekwondo means "the way of the foot and the hand". The History and Traditions of Taekwondo can be traced back into ancient times in Korea. Many of the long-standing traditions are still upheld at Tiger Kim's Academy. At this academy, students learn various forms (Poomsae) from the arts of Taekwondo and Tang Soo Do. They also learn self-defense and sparring techniques which are practiced with a partner. During Taekwondo class, each student wears a white uniform (Do Bok) with the belt of their rank. Beyond the physical techniques, students also learn the traditions of respect and discipline.

Tang Soo Do is another part of Tiger Kim's Academy, many of the techniques and philosophies of Tang Soo Do are the same as those of Taekwondo. Tang Soo Do training also involves the practice of various weapons for increased concentration, exercise and use in competitions and demonstrations. For this reason, Black Belts trained by Grandmaster Tiger Kim and Master Tiger Kim are qualified as Black Belts by the Tiger Kim's Academy, World Taekwondo Federation, Kukkiwon in Seoul, Korea and the World Taekwondo Moo DukGwon."

Q.) Can you explain in your words what Tang Soo Do is?

A.) Tang Soo Do (TSD) is the traditional or classical style of Korean martial arts, also known as Korean karate or super karate because of its high kicks and strong hand techniques. It is the beginning or origin of modern Taekwondo today. TSD is a traditional style art and with that in mind the teachings and techniques today are similar to what was taught back when TSD first originated.

Q.) How long have you been teaching Tang Soo Do?

A.) I have been studying and teaching TSD for over 65 years and having achieved the position of becoming the highest ranked Grandmaster instructor in Denver, Colorado. My academy is located at 1480 Steele St. with a 12,000 sq. ft. training facility, boxing ring, two dojangs, men's and women's locker rooms, Black Belt dressing rooms, martial arts supply store and over 10,000 students have trained at my academy.

Q.) Why did you decide to teach Tang Soo Do over any other form of martial arts?

A.) TSD is what I learned from Grandmaster Hwang Kee. At the time during the occupation most martial arts were banned to be practiced. I wanted to learn Korean martial arts and with this I was fortunate to have been accepted to learn the arts of TSD from the source.

Q.) What are the origins of Tang Soo Do?

A.) TSD began in 1947 with its first school opening in 1955 just after the war. Grandmaster Hwang Kee is the founder of TSD who developed the art into what it is today. TSD originates from the Tang Dynasty and means the way of Tang's open hand. TSD is taught and trained in 45 countries.

Q.) Why can't Tang Soo Do be traced back to a single founder?

A.) TSD can be traced back to Grandmaster Hwang Kee as he was the one who trained myself, and was teaching this martial art. TSD as you know today, he developed, even though it has roots from China, and some of the style from Karate still can be traced back to one source.

Q.) What is the association with Moo Duk Kwan and Tang Soo Do?

A.) MDK is the original name of TSD and was spread as the family of TSD later. Today, MDK is a separate organization from TSD. TSD is the martial arts and MDK is the Headquarters for both TSD and Tae Kwon Do (TKD) today.

Q.) What is the requirement for studying this form of martial arts?

A.) All are accepted, one may begin training by just starting with an open mind and willing body. One must put in the time and energy, and with this will achieve greater harmony within.

Q.) Are there any age ranges that need to be considered for being a student of Tang Soo Do?

A.) At our school, students can begin their training at the early age of three-and-a-half years old.

Q.) Do you have a specific philosophy for the type of Tang Soo Do you teach?

A.) Our philosophy of martial arts is to strive to inspire each and every member to strengthen their mind and body through TSD, and TKD, striving for Black Belt excellence. We work together in providing individualized attention through understanding students' needs and encouraging them to attain their best.

We offer a martial arts curriculum rich in tradition with modern life application. It emphasizes physical skills and development of character to provide lifelong benefits. We provide a family environment that can participate in martial arts together, and a comfortable, supporting atmosphere, which is challenging and empowering.

Q.) Does your school compete professionally?

A.) Yes, we have our students compete in all levels of tournaments at local, state, national and international events. We also host tournaments like the America's Cup, Rocky Mountain National Open and the Colorado State Open championships. These tournaments are open to the public and provide a considerable amount of experience.

Q.) Can you explain one-step sparring in Tang Soo Do?

A.) One step sparring is the most fundamental sparring training, but not the most basic. One trains in the technique as a sequence with a partner and practices these particular defenses against a trained attack in one step.

Q.) Why is free sparring important in Tang Soo Do?

A.) Free sparring is an extremely important part of TSD training. One must pay very careful attention to proper practice. It is essential to approach sparring practice with a solid strategy, a sound technical foundation, a healthy attitude, a good sense of personal discipline and proper etiquette. Sparring is primarily concerned with students exchanging energy in a positive way -- sometimes giving energy (attacking) and sometimes receiving energy (defending). Sparring allows the practitioners to develop combinations and precision timing.

Q.) Why are the commands given in Tang Soo Do similar to those in Tae Kwon Do?

A.) The commands are similar due to the nature of origin, both are from Korea martial arts and it is the native language.

Q.) What are some of the ranking levels of achievements in this form of martial arts?

A.) All students will start with a white belt, yellow belt (8 Geup), high yellow belt (7 Geup). green belt (6 Geup). High green belt (5 Geup), blue belt (4 Geup), high blue belt (3 Geup), red belt (2 Geup), high red belt (1 Geup), bodan (Jr. Black), Black Belt (1 Dan), Black Belt (2 Dan), Black Belt (3 Dan), Black Belt (4 Dan), Black Belt (5 Dan), Black Belt (6 Dan), Black Belt (7 Dan), Black Belt (8 Dan), and the highest is a Black Belt (9 Dan)

Q.) Is there anything you can add that would help a beginner choose Tang Soo Do over any other form of martial arts?

A.) TSD is designed to pass the tradition from one generation to the next to create warriors, not fighters, maintain a truly traditional and professional mentality while teaching a martial art not a sport. Many martial arts abandon many valuable aspects of training in order to gain recognition and notoriety. TSD practitioners strive to maintain traditional values of respect, discipline, self control, self improvement, etiquette and ultimately live a healthy and harmonious life, physically, mentally and spiritually.

Thank you...

If you would like to learn even more about, Tiger Kim's Academy, their information will follow.

Grandmaster Tiger Kim 9th Dan
Tang Soo Do MDK # 123
Tiger Kim's Academy
www.tigerkim.com
info@tigerkim.com
303.388.1408

Wing Chun - Gotham Martial Arts

"Answers Provided By *William Wai-Yin Kwok*"

"Established in 2007, Gotham Martial Arts is a traditional martial arts school that offers both Wing Chun Kung Fu and traditional Taekwon-Do programs in New York City. It is the only official school in America that teaches Grandmaster Wan Kam Leung's Wing Chun system - Practical Wing Chun. The head master, William Wai-Yin Kwok, has 30 years of various martial arts experience and over 10 years of teaching experience. He is Grandmaster Wan's first Closed Door Disciple that has both completed the Kung Fu system and taught professionally outside of Hong Kong. Besides Wing Chun Kung Fu, he trained extensively with internationally acclaimed Taekwon-Do teacher, Grandmaster Kim Suk Jun for over 10 years and earned the rank of Master Instructor. Master Kwok has also earned two Post Graduate Degrees from Harvard University and St. John's University."

Q.) Why did you decide to teach Wing Chun?

A.) I love martial arts, and I wanted to find the one that suited me the best. I have experienced quite a few different martial art disciplines, and before teaching Wing Chun professionally, I had 10 years experience teaching traditional Taekwon-Do. I decided to teach Wing Chun professionally because these days non-Chinese tend to be more interested in learning and teaching Wing Chun than Chinese, so as a native born Chinese from Hong Kong, I felt a responsibility to introduce this scientific and practical martial art to martial art lovers in America, and more importantly, to introduce traditional Chinese culture to the rest of the world.

Q.) What is the association with Wing Chun and Yim Wing Chun?

A.) A Buddhist nun named Ng Mui developed a style of kung fu that was meant to be used in rebellion against the Qing dynasty regime. This kung fu style focused on applying quick and powerful techniques in a short distance. If the techniques can be executed correctly, a practitioner is able to defeat a larger opponent. It was very effective against many traditional martial art styles which tended to have broad movements.

Ng Mui taught this yet unnamed martial art to a young lady called Yim Wing Chun who refused to accept a marriage proposal by the leader of a local gang. This upset gang leader, who was a martial art practitioner and very strong. He challenged Yim Wing Chun in a fight. If Yim Wing Chun lost the fight, she had to marry him. However, Yim Wing Chun won the fight by using the martial skills Ng Mui taught her. Yim Wing Chun married Leung Bok Chau then taught the martial art to her husband, who decided to name it after his wife, "Wing Chun".

Q.) Can you explain the association Yip Man has with Wing Chun in terms of the popularization of this art?

A.) Grandmaster Yip Man was the first to openly teach this secret martial art after he moved from Foshan, China to Hong Kong in 1949. His students, such as Wong Shun Leung (known for rooftop fights to test his martial skill) and Bruce Lee (famous for his martial arts films), made the name of Wing Chun famous not only in Hong Kong, but also internationally. Back then, China was not an open society and Wing Chun was banned in mainland China. However, Hong Kong was a British colony. It was a relatively more open society and an international city that connected the East to the West. Hong Kong residents including many of Yip Man's students had more opportunities and immigrated or traveled to other countries. They were then able to spread Wing Chun throughout the world. For example, my teacher, Grandmaster Wan Kam Leung has been teaching Wing Chun seminars internationally dating back to when Hong Kong was still a British colony. Today, he has many Chinese and non-Chinese students, including me, teaching Wing Chun outside of Hong Kong. Therefore, without Grandmaster Yip Man teaching Wing Chun openly after he moved to Hong Kong, Wing Chun wouldn't be the second most practiced Chinese martial art after Tai Chi today.

Q.) What is the difference between Wing Chun tradition/philosophy and the Western Philosophy?

A.) This is a broad subject. We can go on for days. In short, I would say the Wing Chun tradition is the Chinese Kung Fu tradition. Chinese culture emphasizes respect to teachers and elders. A traditional Chinese martial art school is a family. We use terms such as Sifu (Kung Fu father), Sihing (older Kung Fu brothers), Sije (older Kung Fu sisters), etc. to address each other as a show of respect. Loyalty to your martial art family is very important.

The Chinese term "武術" is translated as "martial arts" or "martial skills". The Chinese character "武" literally means "martial". "武" can be divided into two characters "止" and "弋" which literally mean "cease" and "war". There is an old Chinese saying "止弋為武" which implies "martial art is a skill set that is meant be used to cease war or stop violence". In Sun Tzu's Art of War, he said "To win one hundred victories in one hundred battles is not the highest skill. To subdue the enemy without fighting is the highest skill." As you can see, the philosophy of Chinese martial arts is to promote peace and avoid confrontation. I find one of the major principles of Wing Chun "not using force against force" is in line with the meaning of martial arts we discussed. Although Wing Chun is a very effective close quarter combat martial art, I teach our students to avoid confrontation, if possible, and use our skills only when forced to do so. Wing Chun is a way of life and teaches us important principles of life such as balance of Ying and Yang, courtesy, patience, integrity, self discovery, and perseverance.

On the other hand, these traditions and concepts are not emphasized as much in the Western culture and philosophy.

Q.) Can you explain the philosophy behind the original form of Wing Chun?

A.) Wing Chun can be used with great effect when you only have a small space or fight at close range. Wing Chun uses the body structure to gain power by observing the centerlines, angle, speed and relaxation. Similar to Tai Chi, we begin our training by learning how to relax and generate the soft power. We avoid using force against force in combat. Later in the training, we need to find a balance of hardness and softness. The simplicity and efficiency of Wing Chun teaches us to defend and attack almost simultaneously by smoothly transitioning between techniques so that we have a chance to protect ourselves when we face a much bigger and stronger opponent.

The three forms of Wing Chun - Siu Lim Tao, Chum Kiu and Biu Ji - all have specific advantages and disadvantages. We need to apply the techniques correctly. If a person wants to be proficient in Wing Chun, both of the hands have to be coordinated well. For example, when we begin learning Siu Lim Tao, we start training with one hand first and when we get better we start making two different movements with both hands simultaneously. When we start to feel that coordination between the arms is good and we apply it with speed, it is much easier to react when the opponent launches attacks and to counterattack.

Q.) Is this the only form of martial arts you teach? If so or if not, please explain?

A.) No, I am still involved in teaching traditional Taekwon-Do. But I am teaching fewer lessons now. I don't believe in mixing different martial arts styles; I teach them separately. My personal feeling is that students should not focus on too many styles. I choose to focus more on Practical Wing Chun now because it suits me better - it offers me a lot of room to develop and think. Every practitioner should do a lot of research, find the martial art that suits them best, and stick with it. At a higher level in their martial art journey, they should have a basic understanding of what other martial arts offer, which will improve their understanding of their own martial art. All martial art styles have their benefits and disadvantages. No martial art style is perfect and so I encourage my advanced students to keep an open mind.

Q.) Is the stance, structure and balance of Wing Chun similar to any other form of martial arts?

A.) Generally no. Wing Chun is good for narrow and constrained environments such as elevators, trains, restaurants, urban environments. It is very effective in close-range combat. When Ng Mui developed this martial art, she was thinking of how a petite Chinese woman like herself could fight someone bigger. To do this, the way to generate power will be different than most martial arts system. Other martial arts tend to have broad motions. Wing Chun emphasizes body structure (centerlines, angles and relaxation); practitioners with a better body structure have a higher chance to win a fight. It focuses on the smaller movements in order to be more direct, so that it is quicker. Wing Chun stance is relatively narrow compared to most other martial art styles. Both feet should be equally placed on the ground. The body weight distribution should always be 50% on the left leg and 50% on the right leg. The stance is solid but mobile and deep-rooted but relaxed. Practitioners are trained to use two hands at the same time. We almost always face our target square-on so that both hands are equally useful, especially at close range. We also focus on using one arm to cover both of an opponent's arms. Like many martial arts, relaxation plays a key role in Wing Chun, perhaps even more so. I see this as very similar to martial arts like Tai Chi, where you begin with slow, soft motions, focusing on relaxation. Eventually you want to achieve a balance between hardness and softness.

Q.) Is there any particular age group you teach?

A.) The youngest are pre-teen, the oldest is 65. Students need to be mature enough to understand the concepts of Wing Chun. It is a very scientific martial art, so we always talk about angles and centerlines. Younger people could understand but may get bored because the first form is stationary and movements are slow. Younger children may not have the attention span to stick with it.

Q.) Is there any preparation a beginner needs to consider before becoming a student?

A.) Have a good understanding that martial art training takes time before you see effective results. Many people get excited after seeing a movie and want to be a superhero after two weeks; people have to be realistic. The Chinese term "Kung Fu (功夫)" literally means "hard work and time". I want the student to have faith in the system and the teacher which is why the system and teacher must be researched. They should try different schools. Some schools may offer the same martial art style but with different instruction. They must find where they are comfortable and give themselves time to experience it. Finding the right school and instructor is important.

Q.) Does your school compete professionally?

A.) No. Wing Chun is not meant for competition. It is a martial art created by a woman to finish the fight as quickly as possible. In competitions there are always weight divisions and rules; Wing Chun does not observe those rules as there are no weight divisions when you are walking on the street and encounter a threatening situation. So the techniques we practice may not be suitable to use in competitions. Although some Wing Chun organizations want to promote Wing Chun and create a sport version of it so that more people are interested in the style; however, this was not the original idea of the martial art.

Q.) Are the methods you teach the same as a person would find in a different school teaching Wing Chun?

A.) Everyone has different teaching methods. That is why traditionally, there is always the teacher's name before the martial art, such as "Yip Man Wing Chun" or "Wong Shun Leung Wing Chun". To me, it is important that students understand the teacher's background and teaching methods before they commit to the training. Students need to understand what Wing Chun really is, and why they practice it. I make sure, when a prospective student comes to the school, that they understand what we offer at our school.

Although most Wing Chun schools would teach the core curriculum (three unarmed forms, wooden dummy, long pole, Butterfly knives), some focus more on forms, some more on Chi Sau (a partner training that increases a practitioners' sensitivity), but to me, before a student learns the forms, they have to understand the purpose of Wing Chun and then do the form correctly before they are able to practice partner drills (San Sau).

For example, some teachers will teach the entire Siu Lim Tao form (the first Wing Chun form) in a relatively short period of time, and then they would allow students to practice Chi Sau. In my school, I teach one part of the form, allow students to practice, apply and understand the concepts from that section, and then they move on to the next section. Every single technique in Wing Chun should have a practical application.

This is why students should learn Part 1 and then practice extensively before learning Part 2, and so on. After they learn partner drills, they then learn Chi Sau. Students need to practice the form and San Sau for a few months before they practice Chi Sau. This is because Chi Sau is a partner drill practiced to learn how to change the San Sau techniques, not just to practice sensitivity which is the usual explanation. In order to understand Chi Sau, the student must first understand San Sau; to understand San Sau, they must understand the form. These are all tools to practice the system, but the concepts must be studied and understood to be effective.

Q.) Do you prefer this form of martial arts over any other?

A.) Like I said before, all martial art styles have their benefits and disadvantages. Everyone should find the style that suits them the best. To me, I like Practical Wing Chun because I know I can do it well and it makes a lot of sense. I can practice Wing Chun even when I turn 70 because it is not taxing on the body. It is a very scientific and practical martial art that gives me a lot of room to develop and think. All techniques in the forms serve like different building blocks that can be combined in many different ways. It is interesting to find the most effective and efficient techniques in a certain situation. Some people like Jujitsu - they should focus on Jujitsu. Some people like Karate - they should focus on Karate. It is not best to be a jack of all trades, master of none; focus on one. I like most martial arts systems but I choose to focus on this because it gives me room to think and grow, improving the current system based on original Wing Chun principles and without adding unnecessary stuff.

Q.) How can a person get started with becoming a student of Wing Chun?

A.) When a person goes to different Karate or Shaolin Kung Fu schools, that person might not see a huge difference in the forms. However, when you go to different Wing Chun schools, the forms can be quite different. For those who are interested in studying Wing Chun, I advise them to visit different schools, do research about the Wing Chun lineage of the teacher, and take a trial lesson. They should find a teacher that they are comfortable with and can teach them effectively.

Q.) Does this form of martial arts also help with focus, strength and overall fitness?

A.) Absolutely. Every technique in the form has a practical application so when we practice, we really need to focus on structure, breathing, and relaxation. We need to have a very calm mind when you practice. Don't forget that Wing Chun was created by a Buddhist nun. When we practice the Siu Lim Tao form, it can be almost like meditating. For strength, we learn how to generate lots of power with body structure. Students much bigger than me are amazed at how much power I can generate through my body structure. In terms of overall fitness, exercise does not equal fitness. All forms of exercise, running, weight lifting, etc., can be bad for the body in some ways. Wing Chun is not a hard style, so people are less likely to injure themselves during practice. We also focus on proper breathing which improves blood circulation. By using body structure, we use our body more efficiently and will gain muscle strength, tone and flexibility.

Q.) Can men and women both become students of Wing Chun?

A.) Yes, it was designed specifically to be effective for people of either sex or any size. From my experience, beginners with a more relaxed body may find it easier to start. I find that usually, women take to the idea of relaxing more naturally when first learning the form. Some men do need to learn how to relax properly before their bodies become more accustomed to Wing Chun practice.

Q.) Can you provide any additional details about Wing Chun that may help a person understand more about the art?

A.) While there are DVDs and books on most martial arts, it is not an effective way to learn Wing Chun. Wing Chun is a martial art that emphasizes sensitivity and feeling. That's why Wing Chun has a unique training exercise – Chi Sau. A person could learn the movements from a book or video, but to really understand the unique combat system, it is necessary to feel the teacher's techniques and train with a partner because the techniques are very precise and depend on sensations. It is impossible to advance without a training partner, so to really learn Wing Chun, it is necessary to go to class and have an instructor teach how the concepts apply to movements of the body. Like all other martial arts, it takes a lot of hard work and time to be proficient at Wing Chun, but it must also be the right kind of work in order to get good results.

Thank you...

If you would like to learn even more about, Gotham Martial Arts, their information will follow.

William Wai-Yin Kwok
Wan Kam Leung Practical Wing Chun Kung Fu America
Gotham Martial Arts
info@NewYorkWingChun.com
www.NewYorkWingChun.com
212.326.9510

Chapter 10

Isshinryu Karate – Pro Karate Center

"Answers Provided By *Sensei Dean Lavas*"

"My name is Dean Lavas; I'm a 5th degree Black Belt in Isshinryu karate. I've been training in the martial arts since 1975. I have been studying Isshinryu karate for 18 years. Prior to studying Isshinryu, I studied Okinawan Kenpo. I loved both styles, but Isshinryu was my passion.

I loved Isshinryu so much, that I decided to make it my career.

In 2012, Pro Karate Center was recognized by the AAU (Amateur Athletic Union) as one of the top schools in the country. The Pro Karate Center was awarded the "Best Business in Palm Harbor" by the Palm Harbor patch in 2012.

Since 1975, Pro Karate Center has been providing instruction in Karate and the martial arts in the Palm Harbor, Dunedin, Ozona, East Lake, Tarpon Springs and Clearwater, Florida areas.

The Pro Karate Center provides a safe and family-oriented martial arts experience for students of all ages. Our mission is to foster self-improvement and personal development through focused training. We promote physical fitness and positive social interaction in a courteous and fun atmosphere. Our greatest responsibility is to instill in our students a sense of discipline and a code of ethics to inspire them to lead exemplary lives as leaders in the community. Our purpose is to empower all who desire to accomplish their goals by enabling each to achieve his or her potential. Our mission is to serve our members, their families, and our community by utilizing all of our skills and talents to help you or your child develop himself or herself in a healthy and progressive manor.

Our instructors are dedicated to passing along skills, enthusiasm, and confidence to each and every student. We feel our programs are the best the area has to offer featuring well-organized classes for children, teens, and adults. Pro Karate Center is a sound business and a program our students are proud of.

The Pro Karate Center was established to promote good mental health, physical fitness, and self-defense through the Okinawan style of karate, Isshinryu. Isshinryu's main objective is the perfection of oneself through both mental and physical development. As students learn the art of self-defense, they acquire self-confidence, humility, and the ability to concentrate. Isshinryu combines a well-rounded exercise program with important advantages over other styles.

Headed by Dean Lavas and a staff of expert instructors and managers, including Gary Repetti, and Nathan McKnight. The Pro Karate Center offers a number of programs for physical fitness and instruction in Karate."

Q.) Why did you decide to teach Isshinryu?

A.) Before coming an instructor and the owner of Pro Karate Center, I studied Isshinryu karate for many years. While training, I realized that Isshinryu is much more than punching and kicking, it's about respect and a way of life. The self-defense portion is a bi-product of Isshinryu karate. The main focus is respect!

Isshinryu is a realistic form of self-defense. The traditional kicks are below the waist targeting the groined and knee depending on the kick, and would be able to stop an attacker immediately. A person does not have to have high kicks to be successful with Isshinryu karate. I have a total knee replacement so my days of high kicks are long gone. Don't get me wrong, we do teach high roundhouse and spinning kicks when we're sparring, but not when trying to defend yourself in the street. Kicks to the knee or the groin are much more effective.

I loved Isshinryu karate so much, that I decided to pursue my dream and teach Isshinryu karate as a full time job.

Q.) Why do you prefer this form of martial arts?

A.) When I started out looking for a martial arts school, I was looking for a traditional karate school with roots in Okinawa

Japan, where karate originated. I checked out several schools and styles. I was attracted to Isshinryu because it was a very realistic and close-in self-defense methodology.

- Isshinryu is all about respect and self-discipline.

- Isshinryu's goal is the perfection of oneself through both mental and physical development. As students learn they acquire self-confidence, and humility.

Isshinryu has many advantages over other styles such as:

- Isshinryu *"close-in"* techniques make them more practical on the street and faster to use.

- Isshinryu stances are very natural making them very easy to use in self-defense. There is no wasted motion.

- Isshinryu punches and kicks are snap style, similar to Bruce Lee's philosophy. The reason behind the snap punch and kick is its penetration and power. You can throw a punch or kick with very little reposition of your stance. Your muscles are relaxed until the point of contact delivering a very hard and penetrating punch or kick.

- Isshinryu punch is a little different from other styles; we punch with a vertical fist opposed to a corkscrew punch. The vertical fist is faster to throw and can penetrate to solar plexus without hitting the rib cage.

- Isshinryu also places the thumb on top to make your wrist stronger. When penetrating the solar plexus, you will knock the wind out of your attacker.

- Isshinryu comes from both gojuryu and shorinryu karate, taking the best techniques in each style and incorporating them into Isshinryu.

- All Isshinryu traditional kicks are below the belt, and meant to drop an attacker with one technique targeting the knee or the groin depending on the kick.

Q.) What is the association with Isshinryu Karate and Okinawan Karate?

A.) The association we belong to is called the United Isshinryu Karate Association (UIKA).

The UIKA is made up of Isshinryu practitioners all over the world. Master Harold Mitchum, a 10th degree Black Belt created the UIKA . Master Mitchum was one of the pioneers who brought Isshinryu to the United States from Okinawa Japan. Master Mitchum was Tatsuo Shimabuku's number one American student. Tatsuo Shimabuku was the Soke (founder) of Isshinryu karate.

The UIKA takes pride in doing their katas (forms) and bunkai (application of the forms) the same way Master Shimabuku performed them. The UIKA does everything possible to keep Isshinryu pure and traditional.

We are so very fortunate to have Master Mitchum teach us.

Q.) What is the origin of Isshinryu karate?

A.) Isshinryu karate comes from Okinawa Japan. The Soke or founder of Isshinryu karate was Master Tatsuo Shimabuku. Tatsuo means dragon boy. His birth name was Shinkiche Shimabuku.

Tatsuo Shimabuku was born September 19th 1906 and died on May 30th, 1975. Isshinryu karate was recognized on

January 15th, 1956.

Isshinryu karate comes from Goju Ryu and Shorin Ryu, which Shimabuku studied prior to creating Isshinryu karate. The translation of Isshinryu karate is "One Heart Method". I teach my students that Isshinryu means doing your best at everything you do in life, whether it is practicing Isshinryu karate or doing your homework, do it with your entire heart and give it 100% and you will be successful in life.

Shimabuku and his family were farmers and lived in Kyan Village in Okinawa Japan. Kyan is pronounced "Chun".

Shimabuku was eight years old when he started his training. His first instructor was his uncle EIZO Shimabuku.

Master Shimabuku's three main karate instructors were Master Chotoku Kiyan, Master Chojun Miyagi and Choki Motobu. He learned Goju-Ryu karate from Master Miyagi, and Shorin-Ryufrom Master Motobu and Master Kiyan. Master Kiyan also taught Master Shimabuku weapons, also known as Kobudo.

It was told that Shimabuku would travel to Shuri to do chores in exchange for karate lessons. Each town in Okinawa taught different styles of karate. In Shuri they taught Shuri-te which is known as Shorinryu today. In Naha, the capitol of Okinawa they taught Naha-te, which today is called Gojuryu. All karate styles were once called Okinawa-te, where 'Te' means hand. The word karate means empty hands. The Okinawans had to defend themselves against the Japanese samurai with their "empty hand" karate.

Master Shimabuku learned Kobudo (weapons) from Tiara Shinken.

After years of training Shimabuku was well respected on the island of Okinawa for his karate knowledge. After World War II, Shimabuku opened up a Dojo and began to teach

Isshinryukarate to the US military. This is how Isshinryu and many styles came to the United States. Master Harold Mitchum, Shimabuku's number one American student ran the Dojo in Agena. Master Shimabuku had a contract with the US military to teach the US service men Isshinryu karate.

Master Shimabuku died on May 30th 1975. I don't think Master Shimabuku could have ever imagined how big Isshinryu has grown across the world.

Q.) Is the Kata in this form of Karate different than that of traditional or Western Karate?

A.) Isshinryu Katas are made up of Gojuryu and Shorinryu katas. There is only one kata that is strictly Isshinryu. The Isshinryu versions of the gojuryu and shorinryu katas are different than traditional gojuryu and shorinryu katas. Remember Shimabuku took the best of Gojuryu and Shorinryu and incorporated them in Isshinryu.

There are 8 hand katas and 7 Kobudo or weapon katas. Isshinryu uses three weapons, the BO or stick the SAI and the Tonfa, which is like a police baton.

Kata's are pre-determined defense, attack and counter-attack movements. Kata develops speed, coordination, technique, and accuracy.

There are eight empty hand kata that teach five stances in Isshinryu Karate. In addition, there are three Bo kata, two Sai kata, and one Tuifa Kata.

Empty Hand Kata:

1. *Seisan*: This kata comes from Shorinryu karate. It is known to be one of the oldest katas in traditional styles or karate. This form is the first form you learn in Isshinryu karate. This kata moves in all directions, teaching the karate-ka how to change directions

quickly and proficiently.

2. *Seiuchin*: This kata comes from Gojuryu karate. It is the second kata you learn in an Isshinryu Dojo. This kata works on your horse stance, or known as a Shiko dachi stance. This kata will require leg strength just through the stance alone.

3. *Sanchin*: This kata comes from gojuryu. It's the third kata you learn in an Isshinryu Dojo. Sanchin was created by Master Miyagi. The translation of Sanchin is three conflicts, mind, body and spirit. It teaches the karate-ka correct breathing. It's a relative short kata but very difficult to perform correctly.

4. *Naihanchi*: This kata comes from Shorin Ryu karate. It's the fourth kata you learn in an Isshinryu Dojo. The lateral movement helps you defend yourself if against a wall or on a ledge. It teaches you close-in techniques.

5. *Wansu*: The origin of this kata is from Shorin Ryu. It is known as the dumping kata. One part of the kata is dumping your attacker. This kata is over 300 years old. It consists of 48 karate techniques.

6. *Chinto*: This kata comes from Shorin Ryu. It is an advanced kata and very difficult to perform. Many stances and strikes are incorporated in this kata. Cat stance, crane stances and forward stances. One of the difficulties of this kata is the angles throughout the form.

7. *Kusan-Ku*: This kata originates from Shorinryu. It is the sixth kata that you will learn at an Isshinryu Dojo. Master Kusanku, a Chinese martial artist created this form. It is said to be a kata to defend against eight attackers. There are a lot of up and down movements, which improve the students speed.

8. *Sunsu*: This is the only kata that is strictly Isshinryu.

It is the last form you will learn in an Isshinryu Dojo. Sunsu means strong man after Master Shimabuku. Master Shimabuku was a small man, but very strong hence the name of the kata "Strong Man". Master Shimabuku was able to hammer a nail in a 2x4 with his Schuto (side of his hand). This is a very difficult kata to perform with power and accuracy.

Weapons Kata:

BO kata - The BO is a round staff or stick similar to a broomstick. It was used in Okinawa as a walking stick. The Okinawan's in their infamous wisdom use this to defend themselves against the samurai. They developed three forms with the BO.

9. *Tokomeni No Kun* (Bo #1); this kata is named after Master Tokomeni who created this form.
10. *Urashi Bo* (Bo #2); This form was named after a city in Okinawa called Urashi. This is a very complex form and only taught to Black Belts.
11. *Shishi No Kun* (Bo #3); The kata contains 130 movements combined from the Tokomeni and Urashi BO. It is a very long form and only taught to 2nd degree Black Belts.

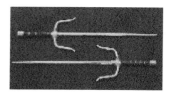

SAI kata - The 'SAI' is a three-pronged weapon. According to some people the sai was a farm tool that the Okinawan's used to plant seeds. It was easy to conceal and carry around in case the Okinawa's were attacked by samurai warriors. They would be able to block a sword, and take it away from their attacker. The Okinawan's carried 3 sai on them at all times. One was for throwing and the other two were concealed in their shirt sleeves. The sai measured the length of their forearm.

12. *Kusan-Ku Sai* (Sai #1); This weapon kata has the same movements as the hand kata Kusan-Ku, but there are no kicks in the weapons kata. This kata is learned at a 1st kyu brown belt.

13. *Chatan Yara No Sai* (Sai #2); This kata originates in the Okinawan city of Chatan. When I visited Okinawa in 1999 we stayed in Chatan. This kata is only taught to Black Belts. It is a very difficult and long sai kata.

Tonfa (Tuifa) Kata

The Tonfa or Tuifa which they call them in Okinawa look like a police night stick. If you've ever watched someone perform the Tonfa, you would bet that the handle moved, but it does not. It is a very difficult weapon to handle. The Okinawan used this weapon to protect themselves against a BO, sai and a sword.

14. Hamahiga No Tuifa); This kata teaches the student to fend off attackers with BOs using blocks and strikes with the tonfas.

Q.) Can you explain some of the upper body basics?

A.) The upper and lower body basics are also known as Kihon (basics). In order to be a proficient karate-ka (student), you must first be proficient with your basics. The basic punches and kicks are a prerequisite to learning kata. It's like learning to read, you must know the alphabet before you can begin to read. Black Belts spend years perfecting their basics. Every class starts off with basic exercises, basic punches and basic kicks.

The main two differences between Isshinryu and other traditional styles of karate is the vertical punch and the position of the thumb. Isshinryu practitioners place their thumb on top to strengthen the wrist. . The thumb is placed on top of the fist rather than wrapping it in front of the fingers like other styles.

There are a total of 15 basic punches.

The benefits of a vertical punch:

1. It's faster and less likely to get jammed.

2. It protects the elbow.

3. It fits into the solar plexus, hence knocking the wind out of your attacker.

Q.) Can you explain some of the lower body basics?

A.) See above answer.

There are a total of 9 basic kicks in the Isshinryu system. Our kicks are very similar of most traditional styles of karate.

Q.) How old does a person have to be to study in your studio?

A.) In our studio we start our little tigers program at age 4, and our oldest adults are 70 years old. It's never too late to start karate lessons. Our Senior instructor at Pro Karate Center started his Isshinryu training at age 40, and is now a 6th Degree Black Belt. You can start at any age. Isshinryu karate is about self-improvement, we do not compare one student against another. It's about the perfection of oneself. Whatever age, you can start your Isshinryu training.

Pro Karate Center codes for our Tiger program (Age 3 to 5)

1. Always do your very best
2. Always follow directions
3. Never punch or kick anyone
4. Never talk to strangers
5. Say NO to drugs
6. Say NO to bullying

We do drills so our Tigers understand the importance of following directions, always doing your very best, and dealing with strangers and bullies.

Pro Karate Center's Student Creeds: This is the backbone of our school:

"I intend to develop myself in a positive manner and to avoid anything that would reduce my mental growth or physical health.

I intend to develop self- discipline in order to bring out the best in myself and others.

I intend to use what I learn in class constructively and defensively; to help myself and my fellow man, and never be abusive or offensive."

Q.) Can this form of martial arts be used for competition?

A.) Isshinryu can certainly be used for competition. In fact, at Pro Karate Center we have over 50 National Champions and 1 World Champion. The circuit that we compete in is the AAU (Amateur Athletic Union). The rules are international rules, and are for all traditional styles of karate such as, Isshinryu, Shotokan, Shorin Ryu, Goju Ryu to name a few. The same rules apply whether you're competing in Okinawa or in Palm Harbor, Florida. Competition is a great tool to better your martial art skills. It's not about winning medals or trophy's, it's about getting better and having fun.

Q.) What are the achievement levels in Isshinryu Karate?

A.) Our Belt rank system is composed of 10 kyu ranks. The word KYU means ranks below Black Belt. When you start you are a 10th kyu White belt and you work through all the levels to become a Black Belt. The kyu ranks descend from 10 to 1, then Black Belt. As you can see from the belts below, the color of the belts get darker as you progress through the ranks. The belt rank system was introduced in the mid 50's. It was a way where practitioners could gauge their progress. Before they had belt ranks in Okinawa, they had one belt, a white belt. The more you practiced the dirtier your belt became. Eventually the belt became black, hence the term Black Belt.

The belt levels are as follows:

- · White Belt 10 kyu
- · Yellow Belt 9 kyu
- · Orange Belt 8th kyu
- · Orange belt with a Blue tip 7th kyu

- Blue Belt 6th kyu
- Green Belt 5th kyu
- Green Belt with a brown tip 4th kyu
- Brown Belt 3rd Kyu
- Brown Belt with a black tip 2nd Kyu
- Brown Belt with 2 black tips 1st kyu
- Black Belt – Sho Dan

Sho Dan is your 1st degree Black Belt. Every degree of Black Belt is called a Dan rank. Interesting that a 1st degree black is called a Sho Dan, the word SHO means beginning. Now that you learned all the basics and kata's it's time to perfect them.

Q.) How long does it take to achieve a master level?

A.) At Pro Karate Center, it takes 4 years of consistent training to become a Black Belt. This is by no means makes you a master. To master Isshinryu, it will take a lifetime.

Q.) How often does a person need to train, based on a typical goal like competing for the first time?

A.) After 6 months of training an individual will learn their first kata and sparring drills. At that point they can compete in kata and sparring at local and national competitions as a beginner. Competition is NOT about winning medals or trophies, it's about learning and improving your martial art skills, and most importantly your sportsmanship, whether you win or lose.

Q.) Do you enjoy teaching this form of martial arts? If so, why?

A.) Teaching Isshinryu karate is the most amazing job in the world. I truly love molding young and older students to be respectful human beings, while making sure they can defend themselves in a bad situation.

It's truly amazing watching these students become respectful, improve in their academics, improve their manners and so on. The parents are so happy and pleased with the education they are getting at Pro Karate Center.

Q.) How long have you been an instructor?

A.) I have been teaching Isshinryu karate full time for 14 years. I have been training in the martial arts since 1975. One of my most memorable moments in my karate career was going to Okinawa Japan with Master Harold Mitchum in 1999. Master Mitchum is a 10th degree black and one of the 4 pioneers who brought Isshinryu to the United States. The biggest things I learned in Okinawa is that karate is a way of life, to be a good respectful moral person. The self-defense portion of Isshinryu is a bi-product of Isshinryu training.

Q.) Can you add any additional information about Isshinryu Karate and why a person would choose this form of martial arts?

A.) The only thing I didn't mention so far is the symbol of Isshinryu. It's called the Mizugami patch, the patch came from a dream that Master Shimabuku had.

The overall meaning of the patch is to stay calm in trouble situations, whether you're being attacked or taking a test in school. Always be calm and prepared. Always move forward. Mizugami's open hand means come in peace and the closed hand means strength or I'll fight if I need to. There are 4 stars on the patch. Three stars represent Master Shimabuku's instructors (Master Kiyan, Master Miyagi and Master Motobu). A fourth star was added for Shimabuku after he died. Master Shimabuku's nickname was Tatsuo. Tatsuo translates to dragon boy. The dragon on the patch represents Master Shimabuku. The kanji or Japanese writing on the patch mean Isshinryu karate-do.

Thank you...

If you would like to learn even more about, Pro Karate Center, their information will follow.

Sensei Dean Lavas
Pro Karate Center
dlavas@tampabay.rr.com
www.ProKarateCenter.com
facebbok.com/prokaratecenter
727.734.9659

Ninjutsu – Kumori Ryu Ninjutsu

"Answers Provided by *Jon R. Duvall*"

"Kumori Ryu Ninjutsu was established in 2008 by Jon R. Duvall and is founded on the historical study and philosophy of Nin. A literal translation of perseverance, endurance, stealth, a sword over the heart... The principals and skills left behind by the Feudal Ninja of Japan were the very essence of Ninjutsu. We take the historical evidence and the translations still remaining for us, to investigate the true ideals of Ninja. In this manner, we can "Recreate" and "Modernize" our approach to Ninjutsu and develop a Life Skill Set that we can share with our future generations."

Q.) What is Ninjutsu?

A.) Ninjutsu is a study, a way of understanding, the realization of inevitability. Ninjutsu as it would be called in feudal eras, is an art passed on by Japans Ninja warriors. Some claim that ninja are black clad assassins of the night that take any job for the right price... Others claim that the samurai were the ones that held the true secrets to Ninjutsu and its (what at the time were) Dark Arts.. We now know through simple research and careful translations that Ninjutsu was in fact a "survival skill set" in addition to the principles and tactics that were recorded to be in use by many for espionage and confrontations in Japan, and at its height during the Sengoku "Warring States" period.

Many are now finding a deeper meaning in "Nin" and are rooting there Mind, Body and Spirit into Ninjutsu training. There are many current or modern Dojo around the world teaching what they consider Ninjutsu. To many it is a recreation of feudal hand to hand and weapons combat techniques used by both the Samurai and Ninja. Collectively the Ninjutsu community believes there are now two sides to Ninjutsu, one is principals and the other skills, which includes "Martial Art". We call our martial form Tai-Jutsu which simply translates to Way of the Body... Through this practice we can watch opponents and observe our surroundings while simultaneously observing their attitude, posture and eventual attack process. We then react appropriately, and in all cases try for escape of the entire situation. Above all Ninjutsu is an art of patience and understanding. Balance, agility, coordination and stamina are all benefits to training Ninjutsu.

Q.) How long have you been a student of the art of Ninjutsu?

A.) 6 yrs.

Q.) How long have you been a master or instructor of this form of martial arts?

A.) 4 yrs.

Q.) What is the relationship with Kain Doshi and Ninjutsu?

A.) We understand that Kain Doshi was a nomad Monk-Warrior that originated from China and had fled to Japan during the conflict in his homelands. In or around 1162, Kain Doshi met Daisuke Togekure, a Samurai that forfeited his lands and power in battle, and instead of facing what samurai call Seppuku, fled to the mountains... It was at that time that they put together a new way of guerrilla warfare tactics and passed it on as what they called Ninjutsu. The way of Nin. Nin is a Kanji used at that time that translates to "to steal in". There is much more historical uncovering that shows us many uses for this Kanji. However, to Kain Doshi and Daisuke Togakure, this is a way of survival on the battlefield and in stealth operations which were vital to Ninja clandestine activities later in Japan.

Q.) In your own words, can you explain the origins of this form of martial arts, as well as the lineage leading to modern Ninjutsu?

A.) There is unfortunately no 100% guarantee that any modern Ninjutsu Dojo will have ties that relate directly to the one true founder of Ninjutsu. We can see that it was built over time by many different individuals that all shared an idea of what they consider to be the proper Ninjutsu. There are many that left different "manuals" that depict Ninjutsu as an art of deception and stealth concepts. In addition there are manuals that refer to Ninja as regular people of different levels of Nin understanding and therefore could fall into a category of a person of Ninjutsu. We believe that these few manuals left behind are the true ways to train in this art and the martial art alleged to be left behind by the Ninja was in fact Samurai arts, which later became Judo and Tai-Jutsu arts as we know and acknowledge today.

Q.) Why are there 18 skills or disciplines in Ninjutsu?

A.) These are the Skills required to survive in the feudal era of Japan, a collection of tools that help Ninja persevere through all that the mission and quite possibly their lives, depend on. A few are very straight forward simple things like horseback riding, geography, swordsmanship and the obvious Tai-Jutsu, but, there are others that require deeper study and greater knowledge of the living world. For example, Ninyaku-Jutsu is a skill set for medicine and earth based remedy for battlefield wounds, animal or insect bites, curing ailments. Overall, these 18 fundamental understandings of your environment will help you live a stronger, better and safer life!

Q.) How young or old does a person have to be to study this form of martial arts?

A.) When one has a need for these skills or ideals then they are ready for training.

Q.) Is this an art both male and females can study?

A.) Indeed!! In fact the female Ninja of Japan were known as Kunoichi. They were the best at infiltration, information collection, spreading confusion and eventual chaos. Ninja in whole rely on a bond of equality that Ninjutsu teaches.

Q.) What does a person need to prepare for when becoming a student of Ninjutsu?

A.) They must open their mind to a life of perseverance, strength, patience, courage and knowing one's mortality... Only then can you understand that living is only important because it ends. The word "Ninja" directly translates to a life of these principals.

Q.) What are some of the weapons and equipment used in Ninjutsu?

A.) Ninja consider all useful items and tools. Weapons no doubt fit into this category. However Ninjutsu practitioners of today use the weapons of the Japanese historical Koryu arts for the most part, these are the Sai, Nunchuku, Tonfa, Bo-staff and Han-Bo. The Ninja-To or Ninja Sword is the most well known weapon and particularly its strait edge design. Shuriken or Ninja Stars are also commonly used in training, which is interesting considering that the Shuriken was a common weapon used by Samurai and many villagers at that time and does not tie directly to Ninja in any known manuals currently translated.

The Knife or Tanto is the weapon of choice for our Ryu because it holds the most current relativity to today's world, knives are used in countless attacks and acts of violence in the streets. Therefore we are prepared.

Q.) Can this form of martial arts be used for competition?

A.) Most of what Ninjutsu contains could not be used legally in a fight of any sanction that I know of.. However I have had sparing sets in which I used plenty of what I had learned training Tai-Jutsu.

Q.) Do you compete in competitions as an instructor or master?

A.) No...

Q.) Is there a ranking system used in Ninjutsu? If so, can you explain what it is?

A.) The alleged "Ranking" system was three levels... Ge-Nin, Chu-Nin and Jo-Nin. The Jo-Nin were leaders of 'Ninja Clans" and passed down orders directly to their Chu-Nin. The Chu-Nin carried out orders and directed Ge-Nin. Ge-Nin were the Ninja foot soldiers of historical Japan. We also know that this three tier system is a way to describe one's understanding and skill level in Ninjutsu. In addition there are also those that fell from order or lost their leaders to enemy encounters. They were known as Ro-Nin.

This creates a four level rank structure used in Kumori Ryu Ninjutsu...
Ge-Nin
Chu-Nin

Jo-Nin

Ro-Nin

Q.) How long does a determined individual need to practice in order to achieve a high ranking in Ninjutsu?

A.) In many modern Ninjutsu schools, a Black Belt status can be achieved in about a 2-3 year time span. However there are many different ranking structures, some schools have 15 levels of rank that practitioners have achieved in 10 to15 years while others have no set time structure and once you can prove skill you are ranked appropriately. In Kumori Ryu you can achieve a Ro-Nin ranking in 3 to 4 years.

Q.) Do you teach any other form of martial arts?

A.) No..

Q.) Do you hold any belts in other forms of martial arts?

A.) No..

Q.) Why did you choose Ninjutsu over any of the other arts currently available?

A.) I was drawn to Ninjutsu because it provides an understanding of an attacker's level of aggression and acknowledges the fact that there are no set guidelines to chaos. I found that Ninjutsu is an ever evolving art that adapts and overcomes. No other Martial Art that I have tried or trained in teaches such a well rounded skill set as Ninjutsu.

Q.) Can you provide any additional information that you feel is important for a new or potential student of Ninjutsu?

A.) Many consider Ninjutsu to be the Martial Arts of Ninja... This is False.. Ninjutsu is separate from Tai-Jutsu which is a general term meaning Martial Art. So please consider when training "Ninjutsu", that it includes much, much more than just "Martial Art". Through a study of all the 18 disciplines, you can unlock great potential in yourself!

Thank you...

If you would like to learn even more about, Kumori Ryu Ninjutsu, their information will follow.

Jon R. Duvall
Kumori Ryu Ninjutsu
Kan-shu / Grand Ro-Nin
www.KumoriRyuNinjutsu.com
KumoriRyuNinja@Gmail.com
719.641.9307

Benchmark Publishing Group

MMA – High Speed Defense

"Answers Provided *by Joe Woo*"

"At High Speed Defense (HSD), our goal is to provide practical real-world martial arts and self-defense training with the utmost efficiency and effectiveness. We do not believe in "styles" or the practice of techniques for the sake of tradition but only what works in the real world. Our no-nonsense approach to the combat arts offers opportunities for the individual to enhance their skills and survivability in the shortest amount of time possible. The training methods employed here are based on real-world practical application of techniques that have been proven through reality. We pride ourselves in offering a facility and instruction that will make our students into well-rounded and complete practitioners."

Q.) What is MMA or Mixed Martial Arts?

A.) MMA or mixed martial arts is a combat sport that has very little restriction on techniques that one can use to win a match. For example, in other combat sports like boxing you are restricted from using elbows, kicks, or hitting below the belt. Or in judo, you are restricted from any strikes such as punches, elbows or kicks. Whereas MMA allows competitors from different combat sports and martial art "styles" to compete on a more level playing field due to the minimum restrictions of techniques. Techniques allowed in MMA include standup striking (punches, elbows, kicks, knees), standup grappling (takedowns, throws, joint locks, chokes), ground grappling (pins, holds, joint locks, chokes) and striking on the ground (punches, elbows, kicks, knees).

Q.) Why did you choose to train in this form of martial arts?

A.) I chose to train martial arts with the goal of learning realistic, self-defense. And training mixed martial arts accomplishes this by allowing me to train all martial art techniques, forms, and "styles".

Q.) How long have you been involved in martial arts in General?

A.) I started training martial arts since I was 8 years old and have been practicing martial arts for over 24 years. I have practiced, competed, and currently teach martial arts.

Q.) What rank do you currently hold as an MMA fighter?

A.) I have fought on a professional level in MMA.

Q.) Although a form of MMA existed in Ancient Greece known as Pankration, why do some associate Bartitsu, Gracie or Brazilian Jiu-Jitsu, and Jeet Kune Do with this form of martial arts?

A.) Those listed styles of martial arts have very similar concepts and theories to MMA. They all approach martial arts in a complete manner by addressing all phases of combat.

Q.) Which of the different styles of martial arts does MMA generally consist of today? And if you teach them, what is your ranking in each of them?

A.) Boxing, Muay Thai, wrestling, submission grappling, kick boxing.

Q.) Can you explain why Kinesiology has become important in MMA?

A.) Kinesiology is important in MMA because it's important to know how the human body functions, how to move your body, how to use your body efficiently and effectively, how to generate power, how joints and limbs can bend and how they can be broken, how to put your body in position to generate power and also how to protect your body from harm. More importantly one must learn how to develop and to improve his or her own strength, speed, power, and stamina needed for MMA.

Q.) What is the general philosophy behind this form of martial arts?

A.) Generally mixed martial artists believe in training to be well-rounded and complete practitioners. And to be able to win a fight in any aspect of combat, either standing up or on the ground via knockout or submission.

Q.) Does your school's philosophy differ?

A.) No we do not differ. We believe in being able to win a fight in any aspect of combat either on the ground or standing up via knockout or submission. Basically by any means necessary to survive dangerous situations.

Q.) How young or old can a person be to study this form of martial arts?

A.) All ages, anyone who is physically able to do the techniques.

Q.) Is this an art that men and women can study?

A.) Yes, men and women can study MMA. There's nothing that will restrict or limit men or women from practicing MMA. In fact, MMA can be a viable means of self-defense for women.

Q.) Do you train all your students for competition or just those that would like to compete?

A.) The techniques in which we teach are applicable in MMA and self-defense. Therefore, all the students that train at our facilities are ready and capable of competing if they chose to do so. We welcome students that choose to train with us for self-defense, competition, physical fitness, or as a hobby.

Q.) What should a beginner consider before choosing MMA?

A.) A beginner should consider what their goals are for training in MMA. Are you ready to work hard? Are you ready to grapple standing up and on the ground? Are you ready to hit others and be hit? Are you ready to take others down and be taken down? A true mixed martial artist needs to be ready to train with an open mind and open to all aspects of combat.

Q.) What are some of the strategies used in MMA?

A.) The strategies used in MMA will depend on the individual practitioner and what their strengths are as far as the different aspects of combat. Some might prefer to fight standing up while others might prefer to fight on the ground. Strategies can also be dependent on the opponent one is facing. If the opponent has relatively weaker stand-up striking skills, then it would be wise to keep the fight in a stand-up striking phase; if the opponent has relatively weaker grappling skills then the fight should be kept in a grappling phase. Strategies can vary greatly depending on the situation presented to the practitioner.

Q.) Why is cross training so important in MMA?

A.) It is crucial to cross train in different skill sets (stand-up striking, stand-up grappling, ground grappling, and ground striking) for MMA because the nature of it requires that the practitioner be able to win and defend oneself in different aspects of combat.

Q.) What type of clothing is required for training and competing in MMA?

A.) For men, MMA shorts and for women, MMA shorts and compression shirt.

Q.) How does the ranking process work in MMA?

A.) MMA doesn't have a traditional ranking process. Instead MMA ranking is based on competition, either on an amateur or professional level.

Q.) What are some of the safety precautions your school implements in order to keep students safe?

A.) Students are asked to wear protective equipment such as a mouthpiece, groin protection, hand wraps, shin guards, gloves and headgear when necessary. We train in a controlled environment with safety in mind.

Q.) Out of the different arts you teach in MMA, will your school grant levels of achievements or ranks for each respective art as each level is mastered or completed?

A.) We do not grant levels of achievement or ranks in our gym.

Q.) Out of the different arts taught and used such as Judo, Jiu-Jitsu, Karate, Muay Thai, Tae Kwon Do, or any others, which are used more consistently than others?

A.) Boxing, wrestling, and submission grappling are used most often.

Q.) Is there anything you can add about MMA that would help a potential student decide on choosing this form of martial arts?

A.) MMA is a combination of effective martial arts techniques. If you want to become a complete martial artist, and to learn all aspects of combat, then MMA is for you.

Thank you...

If you would like to learn even more about, High Speed Defense, their information will follow.

Joe Woo
High Speed Defense
www.highspeeddefense.com
info@highspeeddefense.com
www.facebook.com/HighSpeedDefense
http://www.yelp.com/biz/high-speed-defense-lowell
978.600.8HSD (8473)

CONCLUSION

Congratulations on making it to the end of this book! We hope that you realize and appreciate the immense level of real world knowledge that you've just acquired. The one thing you may be feeling, at this point, is a bit of "information overload", due to the many tips, pieces of advice, and strategies that are jammed into this book. If you are feeling a bit overwhelmed with everything you've just learned, allow us to offer you one final piece of advice: Take a day to let your brain absorb all of the information you just learned. As they say: "Sleep on it". If you attempt to try and remember and implement everything you just learned, your efforts may tend to be scattered and a bit unorganized. Instead, take a day off from the information. If you do this, you're likely to find that you develop a sense of clarity and a better perspective on the information.

Once you've taken a day to allow yourself to re-focus in this way, we encourage you to slowly go back through the book, writing down the actionable information that you intend to implement. Simply reading and understanding the information is not enough. By writing down the information that you plan on implementing, it will allow you to put a clear plan of action into place for yourself.

As you go through the information, don't worry about the order in which you write things down. The first thing to do is to just get the information down on paper. There are many great strategies and tips within this book, but the goal here is for you to extract the exact advice that you will be taking action on. Don't worry if you are unsure about whether or not you will be taking immediate action on certain advice. Just write down everything that you may possibly take action on.

Once you've compiled this list of action steps and "maybe action steps", begin to prioritize this list. In other words, re-write the list with the actions that you know you're going to take at the top of the list and the action items that you may not take action on towards the bottom of the list. By organizing your list in this way, you will be able to build a practical, useable to-do list, from the information you've discovered in this book. Once you've done this, you will be in an excellent position to start taking focused steps, with clarity and purpose.

As we mentioned at the beginning of this book, most people who try Martial Arts do so because of the need for self defense, self discipline and self control. In keeping with the theme of this book, we encourage you to start implementing what you've just learned in this book! Just as we have shared interviews with real world experts who actually do what they talk about in this book, it is our hope that you, as the reader, will take real world action on the information you've learned here.

Wishing you all the best in action-taking, Martial Arts, and a new way of life!

Made in the USA
San Bernardino, CA
11 August 2016